Series Authors
Karen Hume
Brad Ledgerwood

Series Consultants
Jennette MacKenzie, *Senior Consultant*
Damian Cooper, *Assessment*
James Coulter, *Assessment and Instruction*
Gayle Gregory, *Differentiated Instruction*
Ruth McQuirter Scott, *Word Study*

Series Writing Team
James Coulter, *Assessment*
Judith Hunter, *Instruction*
Maureen Innes, *ELL/ESL*
Liz Powell, *Instruction*
Sue Quennell, *Word Study*
Janet Lee Stinson, *Instruction*
Michael Stubitsch, *Instruction*
Giselle Whyte, *Related Resources*

Subject and Specialist Reviewers
Mary Baratto, *the Arts*
Rachel Cooke, *Metacognition*
Phil Davison, *Media Literacy*
Graham Draper, *Geography*
Ian Esquivel, *Media Literacy*
Martin Gabber, *Science and Technology*
Cathy Hall, *Mathematics*
Jan Haskings-Winner, *History*
Maureen Innes, *ELL/ESL*
Dan Koenig, *Health*
Janet Lee Stinson, *Media Literacy*

NELSON / EDUCATION

NELSON EDUCATION

Nelson Literacy 8b

Director of Publishing
Kevin Martindale

**General Manager,
Literacy and Reference**
Michelle Kelly

Director of Publishing, Literacy
Joe Banel

Publisher
Rivka Cranley

Managing Editor, Development
Lara Caplan

Senior Product Manager
Mark Cressman

Senior Program Manager
Diane Robitaille

Developmental Editors
Barbara Muirhead
Marilyn Wilson

Assistant Editor
Adam Rennie

Bias Reviewer
Nancy Christoffer

Editorial Assistant
Meghan Newton

**Executive Director, Content
and Media Production**
Renate McCloy

**Director, Content
and Media Production**
Carol Martin

Production Editors
Janice Okada
Natalie Russell

Copy Editor
Linda Jenkins

Proofreader
Linda Szostak

Production Manager
Helen Jager Locsin

Production Co-ordinator
Vicki Black

**Director, Asset Management
Services**
Vicki Gould

Design Director
Ken Phipps

Managing Designer
Sasha Moroz

Series Design
Sasha Moroz

Series Wordmark
Sasha Moroz

Series Cover Design
Sasha Moroz
Glenn Toddun

Cover Design
Courtney Hellam
Sasha Moroz

Interior Design
Carianne Bauldry
Jarrel Breckon
Nicole Dimson
Courtney Hellam
InContext Publishing Partners
Jennifer Laing
Sasha Moroz
Jan John Rivera
Bill Smith Design

Art Buyer
Suzanne Peden

Art Coordinator
Renée Forde

Compositor
Courtney Hellam

Photo Research and Permissions
Nicola Winstanley

Printer
Transcontinental Printing

COPYRIGHT © 2008 by Nelson Education Ltd.

ISBN-13: 978-0-17-611398-8
ISBN-10: 0-17-611398-3

Printed and bound in Canada
2 3 4 11 10 09

For more information contact Nelson Education Ltd., 1120 Birchmount Road, Toronto, Ontario, M1K 5G4. Or you can visit our Internet site at http://www.nelson.com

Series Advisers and Reviewers

Gwen Babcock, Limestone DSB, ON
Jennifer Bach, Burnaby SD, BC
Karen Beamish, Peterborough, Victoria, Northumberland, and Clarington CDSB, ON
Mary Cairo, Toronto CDSB, ON
Maria Carty, Annapolis Valley Regional SB, NS
Joanna Cascioli, Hamilton-Wentworth DSB, ON
Janet Charlton, District 10, NB
Vivian Collyer, Sooke SD, BC
Anne Converset, Niagara DSB, ON
Rachel Cooke, Toronto DSB, ON
Phil Davison, Halton DSB, ON
Connie Dersch-Gunderson, Livingston Range SD, AB
Lori Driussi, Burnaby SD, BC
Judy Dunn, Kamloops/Thompson SD, BC
Eileen Eby, Greater Victoria SD, BC
Ian Esquivel, Toronto DSB, ON
Anna Filice-Gagliardi, Toronto CDSB, ON
Patty Friedrich, London DCSB, ON
Charmaine Graves, Thames Valley DSB, ON
Colleen Hayward, Toronto CDSB, ON
Irene Heffel, Edmonton SD, AB
Phyllis Hildebrandt, Lakeshore SD, MB
Brenda Lightburn, Mission SD, BC
Andrew Locker, York Region DSB, ON
Susan MacDonald, Delta SD, BC
Anne Marie McDonald, Limestone DSB, ON
Beverley May, District 2, NL
Selina Millar, Surrey SD, BC
Wanda Mills-Boone, Ottawa-Carleton DSB, ON
Lorellie Munson, York Region DSB, ON
Barb Muron, Toronto CDSB, ON
Linda O'Reilly, Educational Consultant, BC
Cathy Pollock, Toronto DSB, ON
Gina Rae, Richmond SD, BC
Sherry Skinner, Eastern SD, NL
Susan Stevens, Peel DSB, ON
Janet Lee Stinson, Simcoe County DSB, ON
Melisa Strimas, Bruce-Grey CDSB, ON
Elizabeth Stymiest, District 15, NB
Sue Taylor-Foley, South Shore Regional SB, NS
Laurie Townshend, Toronto DSB, ON
Tracy Toyama, Toronto DSB, ON
Deborah Tranton-Waghorn, Ottawa-Carleton DSB, ON
Ann Varty, Trillium Lakelands DSB, ON
Ruth Wiebe, Chilliwack SD, BC
Mark Wilderman, Saskatoon Public SD, SK
Nadia Young, Toronto CDSB, ON

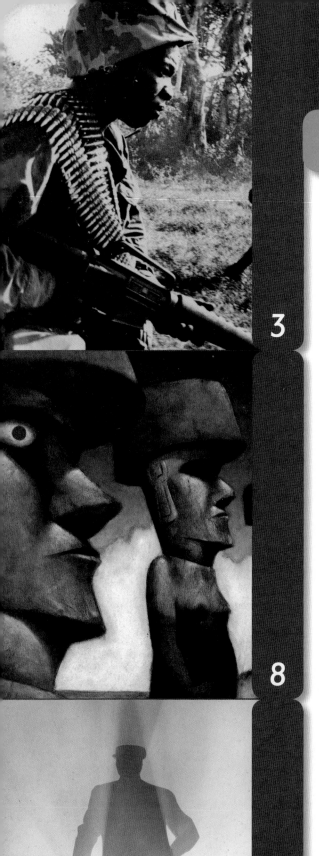

CONTENTS

Unit 3 — Secrets

72

77

84

CONTENTS

Unit 4 — No Limits

92

96

103

Welcome to
Nelson Literacy

Nelson Literacy presents a rich variety of literature, informational articles, and media texts from Canada and around the world. Many of the selections offer tips to help you develop strategies in reading, oral communication, writing, and media literacy.

Here are the different kinds of pages you will see in this book:

Focus pages

These pages outline a specific strategy and describe how to use it. Included are "Transfer Your Learning" tips that show how you can apply that strategy to other strands and subjects.

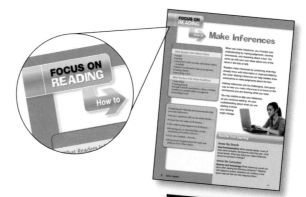

Understanding Strategies

These selections have instructions in the margins that help you to understand and use reading, writing, listening, speaking, and media literacy strategies.

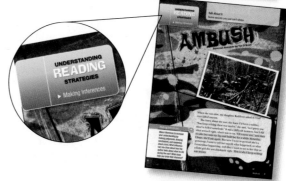

Applying Strategies

These selections give you the chance to apply the strategies you have learned. You will see a variety of formats and topics.

Transfer Your Learning

At the end of the unit, you'll have a chance to see how the strategies you have learned can help you in other subject areas such as Science and Technology, Geography, History, Health, Mathematics, and the Arts.

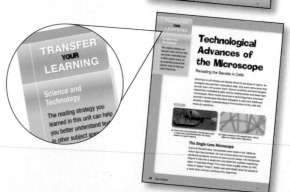

SECRETS

What are some good reasons for keeping secrets?

Unit Learning Goals

- make inferences while reading
- add voice to informational writing

- make inferences while listening
- create comics

- analyze generalization text pattern

Transfer Your Learning: Science and Technology

FOCUS ON READING

How to Make Inferences

What Readers Infer About Fiction

- moral
- setting
- characters' traits, moods, motivations, values, or beliefs
- author's or characters' bias or perspective
- missing details
- preceding events

What Readers Infer About Nonfiction

- main ideas
- missing details
- people's moods, motivations, values, or beliefs
- author's or people's bias or perspective
- preceding events

Completing the following statements may also help you make inferences:

- My own experience tells me the author thinks ...
- I know how the author feels because ...
- The evidence that supports my thinking is ...
- By leaving out, or only including, certain information the author tells me ...
- I can now conclude ... because ...
- My personal viewpoint about the topic may influence how I think about ...

When you make inferences, you increase your understanding by making judgments, drawing conclusions, and reasoning about a text. You come up with your own ideas (about any of the items in the lists at left).

Readers make inferences by combining what they already know with information or clues provided by the writer. Making inferences can help readers draw conclusions or make judgments about the text.

Making inferences can be challenging. One good way to help you make inferences is to focus on the conclusions you are drawing while you read.

You may confirm or alter your inferences as you continue reading. As your understanding about what you are reading evolves, your thinking might change.

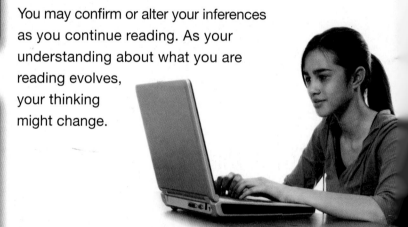

Transfer Your Learning

Across the Strands

Oral Communication: When people speak, much of their communication lies beyond what they say—their actual words. What else helps you make inferences about the speaker's feelings?

Across the Curriculum

Science and Technology: What inferences would you draw after reading the following sentence? "Patients with digestive system disorders can swallow a new space-age pill that will help diagnose them."

Talk About It
Some secrets you just can't share.

AMBUSH

Personal Anecdote by Tim O'Brien

Making Inferences →

Make inferences to increase your understanding by making judgments, drawing conclusions, and reasoning about a text. What inference can you draw about how the author feels about what he did during the war? What clues help you draw that inference?

When she was nine, my daughter Kathleen asked if I had ever killed anyone.

She knew about the war; she knew I'd been a soldier. "You keep writing these war stories," she said, "so I guess you must've killed somebody." It was a difficult moment, but I did what seemed right, which was to say, "Of course not," and then to take her onto my lap and hold her for a while. Someday, I hope, she'll ask again. But here I want to pretend she's a grown-up. I want to tell her exactly what happened, or what I remember happening, and then I want to say to her that as a little girl she was absolutely right. This is why I keep writing war stories.

He was a short, slender young man of about twenty. I was afraid of him—afraid of something—and as he passed me on the trail I threw a grenade that exploded at his feet and killed him.

Or to go back.

Shortly after midnight we moved into the ambush site outside My Khe. The whole platoon was there, spread out in the dense brush along the trail, and for five hours nothing at all happened. We were working in two-man teams—one man on guard while the other slept, switching off every two hours—and I remember it was still dark when Kiowa shook me awake for the final watch.

The night was foggy and hot. For the first few moments I felt lost, not sure about directions, groping for my helmet and weapon. I reached out and found three grenades and lined them up in front of me; the pins had already been straightened for quick throwing. And then for maybe half an hour I kneeled there and waited. Very gradually, in tiny slivers, dawn began to break through the fog, and from my position in the brush I could see ten or fifteen metres up the trail.

The mosquitoes were fierce. I remember slapping at them, wondering if I should wake up Kiowa and ask for some repellent, then thinking it was a bad idea, then looking up and seeing the young man come out of the fog. He wore black clothing and rubber sandals and a grey ammunition belt. His shoulders were slightly stooped, his head cocked to the side as if listening for something. He seemed at ease. He carried his weapon in one hand, muzzle down, moving without any hurry up the centre of the trail. There was no sound at all—none that I can remember. In a way, it seemed, he was part of the morning fog, or my own imagination, but there was also the reality of what was happening in my stomach.

Making Inferences →

To make inferences, combine clues in the text with your prior knowledge. What war do you think is the setting for this story? What clues in the text or photos make you think so? As you read, confirm or alter this inference.

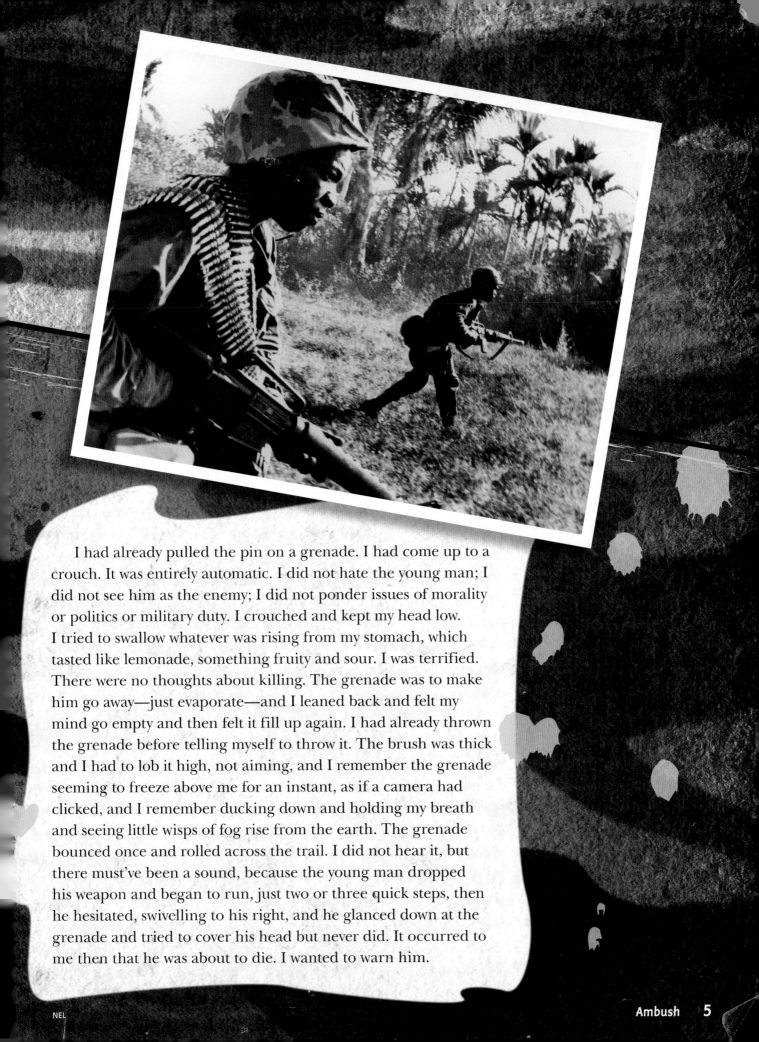

I had already pulled the pin on a grenade. I had come up to a crouch. It was entirely automatic. I did not hate the young man; I did not see him as the enemy; I did not ponder issues of morality or politics or military duty. I crouched and kept my head low. I tried to swallow whatever was rising from my stomach, which tasted like lemonade, something fruity and sour. I was terrified. There were no thoughts about killing. The grenade was to make him go away—just evaporate—and I leaned back and felt my mind go empty and then felt it fill up again. I had already thrown the grenade before telling myself to throw it. The brush was thick and I had to lob it high, not aiming, and I remember the grenade seeming to freeze above me for an instant, as if a camera had clicked, and I remember ducking down and holding my breath and seeing little wisps of fog rise from the earth. The grenade bounced once and rolled across the trail. I did not hear it, but there must've been a sound, because the young man dropped his weapon and began to run, just two or three quick steps, then he hesitated, swivelling to his right, and he glanced down at the grenade and tried to cover his head but never did. It occurred to me then that he was about to die. I wanted to warn him.

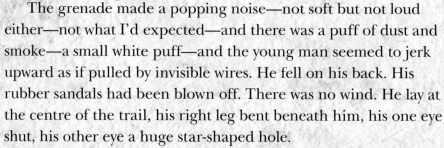

The grenade made a popping noise—not soft but not loud either—not what I'd expected—and there was a puff of dust and smoke—a small white puff—and the young man seemed to jerk upward as if pulled by invisible wires. He fell on his back. His rubber sandals had been blown off. There was no wind. He lay at the centre of the trail, his right leg bent beneath him, his one eye shut, his other eye a huge star-shaped hole.

It was not a matter of live or die. There was no real peril. Almost certainly the young man would have passed by. And it will always be that way.

Later, I remember, Kiowa tried to tell me that the man would've died anyway. He told me that it was a good kill, that I was a soldier and this was a war, that I should shape up and stop staring and ask myself what the dead man would've done if things were reversed.

None of it mattered. The words seemed far too complicated. All I could do was gape at the fact of the young man's body.

Even now I haven't finished sorting it out. Sometimes I forgive myself, other times I don't. In the ordinary hours of life I try not to dwell on it, but now and then, when I'm reading a newspaper or just sitting alone in a room, I'll look up and see the young man coming out of the morning fog. I'll watch him walk toward me, his shoulders slightly stooped, his head cocked to the side, and he'll pass within a few metres of me and suddenly smile at some secret thought and then continue up the trail to where it bends back into the fog.

Making Inferences →

Making inferences can help readers draw conclusions or make judgments. What conclusions can you draw about how the author feels? What evidence supports your conclusions?

Making Inferences →

You may confirm or alter your inferences as you continue reading. Does reading this paragraph make you confirm or change any earlier inferences? Explain.

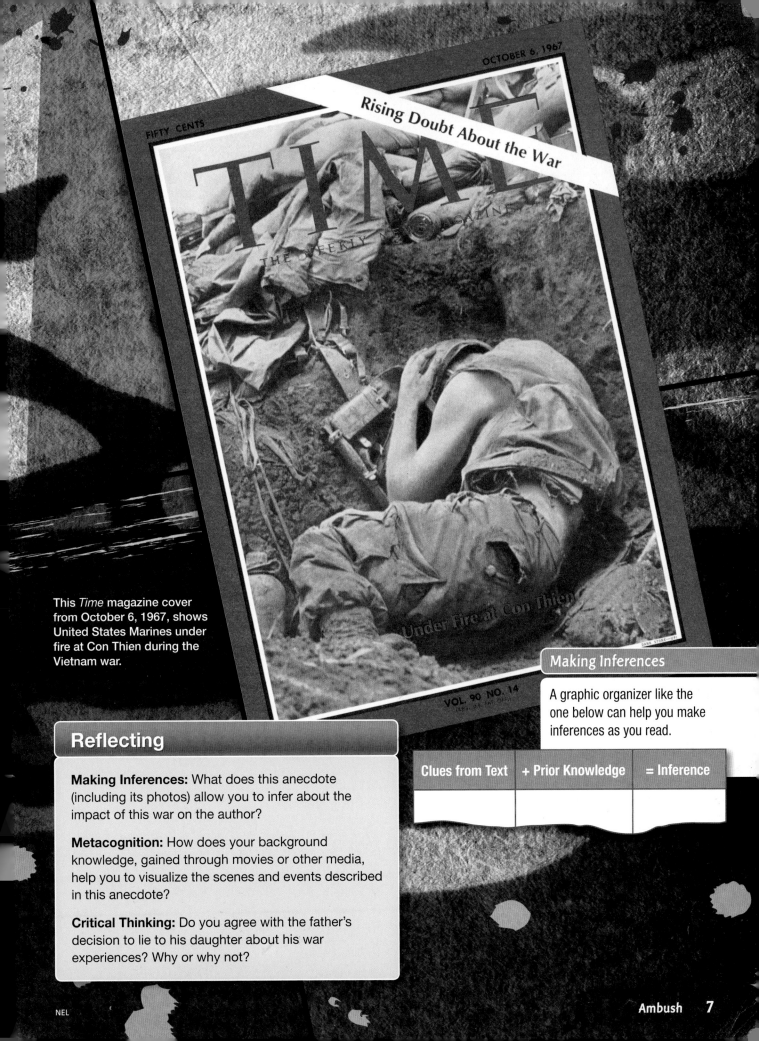

OCTOBER 6, 1967

FIFTY CENTS

TIME

THE WEEKLY NEWS MAGAZINE

Under Fire at Con Thien

VOL. 90 NO. 14

This *Time* magazine cover from October 6, 1967, shows United States Marines under fire at Con Thien during the Vietnam war.

Making Inferences

A graphic organizer like the one below can help you make inferences as you read.

Clues from Text	+ Prior Knowledge	= Inference

Reflecting

Making Inferences: What does this anecdote (including its photos) allow you to infer about the impact of this war on the author?

Metacognition: How does your background knowledge, gained through movies or other media, help you to visualize the scenes and events described in this anecdote?

Critical Thinking: Do you agree with the father's decision to lie to his daughter about his war experiences? Why or why not?

Talk About It
What secrets can stone reveal?

Secrets of

Easter Island

Poem by Jane Yolen

Eyes of stone stare
unblinking in the sun's fierce glare.
Heads of stone ride burial walls
like terns atop
the rise and fall of an ocean wave.
Whose hands did carve,
did care, did save,
did pry, did live, did die
to pull these gods
from the crater's well?
Only mouths of stone can tell.

the Past

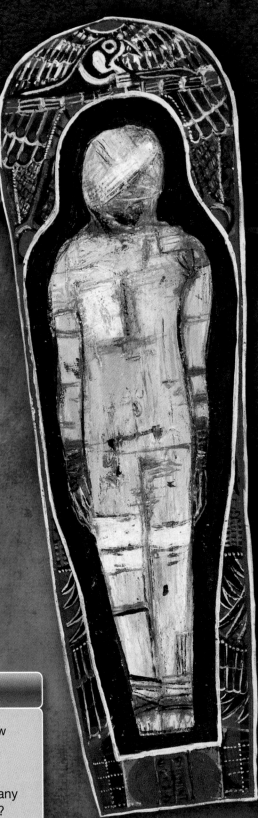

Mummy

Poem by Myra Cohn Livingston

So small a thing
This mummy lies,
Closed in death
Red-lidded eyes,
While, underneath
The swaddled clothes,
Brown arms, brown legs
Lie tight enclosed.
What miracle
If he could tell
Of other years
He knew so well;
What wonderment
To speak to me
The riddle of
His history.

Reflecting

Making Inferences: From the poems, what do you infer about how the poets feel about these ancient wonders? What clues help you make inferences?

Metacognition: How did making inferences help you understand any unfamiliar words in the poems? What other strategies did you use?

Critical Literacy: What is the message of these poems? How do illustrations and *layout* (how text and images are laid out on the page) contribute to the message?

Talk About It
What feelings do you associate with the word *homecoming*?

Homecoming

Science Fiction by Stephen David

At the beginning and end of the typhoon season, when the winds were rising and falling, you could use the current to glide between the Cities in a flitter with its small motor turned off. The favoured game was to ignore the flight decks and glide straight in at one of the portals, swooping over the galleries and terrifying the people walking there. Naturally, this was extremely dangerous. If you missed the portal, the impact with the City's hull could kill you; if it didn't, the two-kilometre drop to the ground probably would. It was a very popular game, and though it wasn't illegal to turn your motor off, it was very illegal to fly in populated areas of the Cities.

Jann had never played the Game. The idea of hurtling through the air with nothing between him and the ground was terrifying. He sometimes had nightmares of falling, hurtling down, seeing the twin Cities towering above him, then turning over in the air to see the ground and the waving heads of the tall fever trees spinning crazily beneath him. Each time, he would wake, sometimes shouting.

It was just such a dream that woke him one night. He padded quietly into the tiny kitchen.

"I had the dream again," Jann said. He climbed on the stool next to his father's.

"The falling dream?" Jann nodded. This was the fifth time since the typhoons had started.

"Well," his father said, "you'd better stay up till the dream's gone. Look." He pointed at the viewing screen. "They're showing the liftoff simulations." On the screen, a computer image showed the City slowly revolving. Down the side of the screen, a scale showed that from base to top the City was just over two kilometres high. Narrow at the base, it broadened out to the kilometre-deep cylinder that housed the living and industrial areas, then tapered again toward the top where the command centres were. Coloured arrows showed the wind direction. At first, the arrows moved slowly, then gradually got faster. The City was spinning, like a top, the speed of rotation increasing as the thrust motors augmented the wind's effect. Again the speed increased, and again, until the lines of the City were a blur. Then it was moving forward and upward, its rotation forcing it out to break free of the planet's weak gravity. Instead of sailing majestically a kilometre or so above the surface, harvesting as many of the fever trees as they could, the Cities would finally break free entirely and sail where those who had built them had intended them to go: into space, into the galaxy—and home. The long exile would be over.

"When will we go?" Jann asked.

"Next typhoon season," his father said. "We need another half-year's good harvesting, then we'll have supplies to last us years in space."

Jann frowned. "Tomas didn't want us to go."

"I think Tomas was just repeating what his parents said."

"No," said Jann, irritated. "He thought a lot about it. He said we'd been here hundreds of years and no one on Earth would remember us, and even if we got back there we wouldn't be happy. He said we should just build small ships and send a few people back to make contact. There must be lots of inhabited planets by now, and we wouldn't have to go all the way back to Earth before finding one."

"No," said his father, with an air that Jann knew meant the discussion was over, "there would be no point. This planet will never be a good place to live. We don't want to spend our lives trapped in these floating Cities—and even if I have to, there's no reason for you to. In my lifetime or yours, we've got to go Home, back where we belong. And it's a long journey. On a small ship, the crew might be dead of old age before they got anywhere."

"Well," said Jann, "Tomas is staying."

"Tomas is dead, Jann," his father said softly. "He played the Game and he fell. No one could survive that."

"No," said Jann. "I suppose not." He slid off the stool and went back to his bunk and a dreamless sleep.

The typhoon roared on. From the Cities to the horizon, little could be seen through the clouds of reddish pollen blown by the shrieking gales. The preparations for the Return continued.

Slowly the winds dropped. The quiet season came, and the harvesting went on. People continued to talk. Every evening, Jann would listen to his parents discussing the departure. He thought about Tomas, his friend, who would not be going.

There came a day when the winds began to rise again. Standing in the vast gallery that overlooked the space between his City, City One, and City Two, Jann could see the first flitters swoop through the early pollen clouds, wheeling and circling before dropping toward the flight decks or portals of the City. That was the way Tomas had gone. No one had seen it happen, but he had left City One and was never seen again. His name was added to the list of victims of the Game; his family and friends mourned him. And Jann wondered. He wondered because when it happened he had not been surprised. While some of Tomas's friends argued about whether he had smashed into the City's hull or lost control and plummeted to his death, Jann thought of the conversation he and Tomas had had only a few days before Tomas disappeared.

"But Tomas," Jann had said, "everyone else seems to agree we've got to go. Surely people wouldn't go on believing something that's not true for so long?"

"Everyone? No, not everyone. I'll tell you who doesn't agree. The harvesters don't agree. And those of us who play the Game don't agree. Now, why should that be?" The harvesters were those who used the flitters for their real purpose— gathering the pulpy fruit of the vast fever trees, which the Cities converted into almost every kind of eating and drinking material. Jann shook his head, and Tomas went on, "Because we're the ones who go outside and look at the planet. The harvesters get right down to the surface, almost, and we at least smell the air and feel the wind on our faces. Jann, this planet is beautiful!"

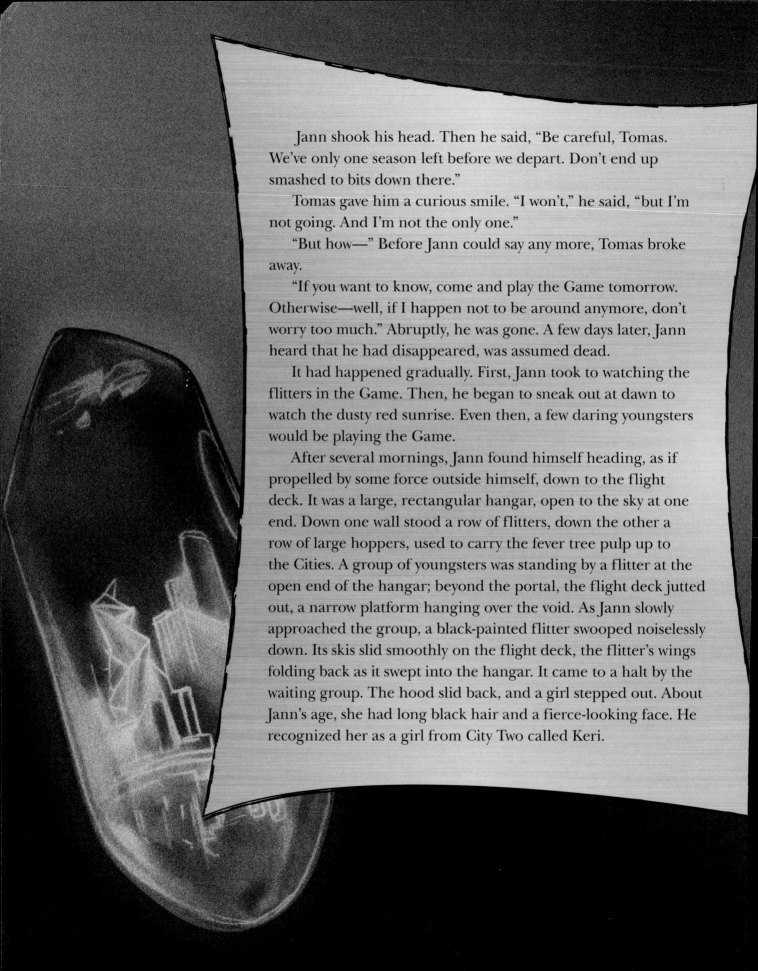

Jann shook his head. Then he said, "Be careful, Tomas. We've only one season left before we depart. Don't end up smashed to bits down there."

Tomas gave him a curious smile. "I won't," he said, "but I'm not going. And I'm not the only one."

"But how—" Before Jann could say any more, Tomas broke away.

"If you want to know, come and play the Game tomorrow. Otherwise—well, if I happen not to be around anymore, don't worry too much." Abruptly, he was gone. A few days later, Jann heard that he had disappeared, was assumed dead.

It had happened gradually. First, Jann took to watching the flitters in the Game. Then, he began to sneak out at dawn to watch the dusty red sunrise. Even then, a few daring youngsters would be playing the Game.

After several mornings, Jann found himself heading, as if propelled by some force outside himself, down to the flight deck. It was a large, rectangular hangar, open to the sky at one end. Down one wall stood a row of flitters, down the other a row of large hoppers, used to carry the fever tree pulp up to the Cities. A group of youngsters was standing by a flitter at the open end of the hangar; beyond the portal, the flight deck jutted out, a narrow platform hanging over the void. As Jann slowly approached the group, a black-painted flitter swooped noiselessly down. Its skis slid smoothly on the flight deck, the flitter's wings folding back as it swept into the hangar. It came to a halt by the waiting group. The hood slid back, and a girl stepped out. About Jann's age, she had long black hair and a fierce-looking face. He recognized her as a girl from City Two called Keri.

"Tomas said you'd come in the end," she said.

"What did he mean?"

"About what?"

"About staying here. And not being the only one."

"Why don't you ask him?"

"How can I?" Jann was fast getting furious. "He's dead!"

"If you really think that," she said slowly and emphatically, gazing for the first time into his eyes, "why are you here?" Furiously, he grabbed her arm, but she pulled away and set off down the hangar. He followed her.

"Every question I ask, you ask me one back. I'm his friend. Where is he?"

She did not break her stride. "Are your family going?" she asked.

He was bewildered. "Going? Of course. Everyone is."

"Tomas isn't."

"But he's—" A terrible thought struck Jann for the first time. "You mean he's alive … down there, on the surface?" She didn't answer. "But if he is, then they ought to send a rescue party, get him back. He'll die. Maybe he's hurt. And the fever trees … he'll get the fever.…" His voice had risen, and he was suddenly aware that he was shrieking.

"Jann, it's a matter of trust." Keri knelt down, her voice low. "Tomas wanted you to come out with us, he wanted to tell you … what was happening. But you wouldn't come, so he wasn't allowed to say anything. He still wants to talk to you, but you've got to give something in return. You've got to make the trip. Then he'll tell you everything."

Jann knew well enough how to do it. He'd spent many hours in the huge free-fall chambers at the top of the City, piloting a flitter in the artificial winds, secure in the knowledge that if anything went wrong, an automatic safety device would immediately land machine and pilot softly and safely. This, though, would not be recreation. He thought of his dream. Keri was watching him closely.

"If you don't," she said, "you'll never see Tomas again." Weakly, he nodded, feeling sick and afraid.

Somehow, when they got back to the hangar, the portal at the far end seemed menacing, and Jann imagined he could see the unpredictable winds gusting past. He thought of the emptiness below the flight deck and shuddered. Keri pointed him toward a flitter.

"I'll keep beside you," she said. "Mostly, once we're out there, we open the hoods. The air's thin but breathable. You don't have to, but I'd recommend it. What you do have to do is switch the motor off."

For the first time in his life, Jann saw a landscape without a city floating above it. He was now only a thousand metres up and could see below him a large patch of fever trees. Beyond them was a flat expanse of something that glinted, from which a silver ribbon wound across the flat, reddish landscape. There was no sound except for the rush of wind. Spiralling below him, he could see Keri's flitter.

Only a minute later, they were below the level of the fever trees, whose odd, bulbous shapes strangely echoed the shapes of the Cities that floated above them. Below the bulbous plants sprouted the sharp leaves, metres across, that gave the trees their name.

There, standing at the edge of the grove of fever trees, were Tomas and his parents.

It was quiet and peaceful in the shade of the trees. The leaves rose for some metres, leaving enough space beneath them for the small settlement of huts constructed from the fibre of the trees. In the foliage above, small creatures chattered comfortably, clicking their tongues in a dozy, muttering way. Beyond the edge of the grove, past the two flitters, water lapped gently on the stony shore, reflecting the starlight. There was a soft murmur of voices as people talked after the evening meal. Jann was sitting with Keri, and with Tomas and his parents outside their hut.

Tomas said, "We're not going. This is our home."

"I thought it was all hostile," Jann said, "and the leaves of the plants, and the pollen—people died."

"At first," said Tomas's father. "People who touched the leaves got fever and died after terrible hallucinations. But we soon became resistant: it's been hundreds of years since a death. But people weren't willing to try. They'd left Earth in a colony ship because Earth was so overcrowded, it was choking to death. They were full of dreams, obsessed with finding a fresh planet, one where clear streams ran through green meadows and high mountains sparkled against a clear blue sky. But one ship, carrying a thousand colonists, had an accident. An asteroid damaged it so badly, it lost contact with the others and had to seek refuge on the nearest planet." He paused. "Here. And what did they find? Lots of stony ground and the fever trees. Within days there were deaths. They stayed in the ship, trying to repair it—and failed. They were stuck on a planet that was the opposite of all they had hoped for."

The groups of people around the huts had fallen silent, listening now. *They must all know the story,* Jann thought, *but they need to hear it again.*

"It was hard at first, just surviving. But in the ship they had all they needed to make the most of any planet they were on. They had mining equipment, laboratories, computerized factories, flitters, you name it. The one thing they didn't have was the capacity to build a new fusion plant to get them off the planet.

"Now, the idea was that when they landed, they'd build a town and start making the planet a good place to live. But what our ancestors did instead was to bed down in the disabled colony ship and start figuring out ways to get away.

"They'd only been here a month or so when the typhoon season started. They weren't ready for it, so that halved the population. But when it was all over, one of them remembered something he'd seen …" Tomas's father paused dramatically and gestured upward. "As the winds built up, the fever trees began spinning. And just when the typhoon started, they spun so hard they took off into the sky, flinging pollen every which way."

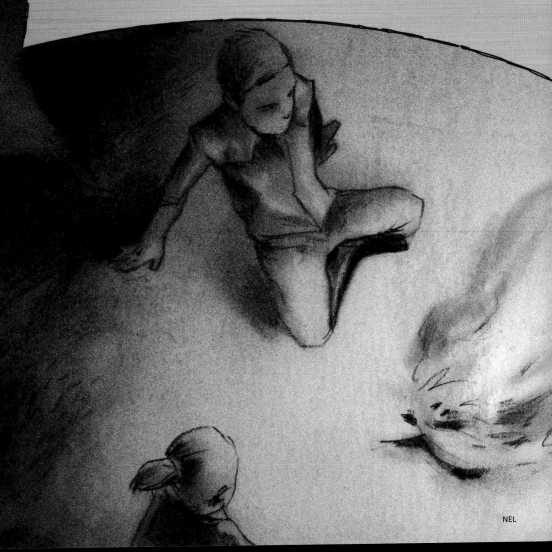

"So there is a reason why the shapes look the same," Jann exclaimed.

"It's the same principle. The planet's got low gravity, and that typhoon can act like a whip on a spinning top. Mind you, it took hundreds of years. The first cities were top heavy. They crashed. It was only about four generations ago that One and Two finally became habitable."

"They'll leave without you," Jann broke in. Around him, the family smiled. Tomas gestured at the group of huts, the people sitting quietly in their doorways in the warm air, the soft murmur of conversation.

"Yes," he said quietly, "but they're leaving us in our home. Jann, people have been slipping away from the Cities for some time now. We aren't the only settlement. We know this planet isn't paradise but there is enough to eat, and we will survive and, in the end, we will cultivate it and build towns and, one day, even cities. Jann, stay with us."

"I've got to go," Jann said. "All my life I've lived with the dream of all of us going back into space and finding the rest of the human race. There must be lots of planets by now with people on them. We seem so—cut off here. Nothing's happened here, ever."

"Jann," said Tomas gently, "that's because the people who wanted to leave wouldn't let anything happen."

"Well," said Jann, "yes, but I must go. I like your world, but I must go."

Reflecting

Making Inferences: What inferences did you make about Jann's character? How did those inferences change over the course of the story? What clues or prior knowledge helped you make inferences?

Metacognition: What personal connections did you make as you read? How did those connections help you to understand the relationship between Jann and Tomas?

Connecting to Other Media: Which media form would be most effective for creating a visual representation of this story—a comic strip or a movie? Why do you think so?

Talk About It
What do you already know about Jewish ghettos and internment camps during World War II?

My Secret Camera

Photo Essay by Mendel Grossman and Frank Dabba Smith

This photo shows Mendel Grossman at work in his darkroom.

Life in the Lodz Ghetto

Mendel Grossman was born in Poland in 1913. In 1940 he, along with his family, was confined to the Lodz Ghetto. There he secretly produced thousands of photos of life in the ghetto, distributing them widely and hiding the best negatives in the wall of his apartment. Tragically, he died in 1945, just days before the Germans surrendered.

I have a secret camera. I hide it under my raincoat. I have cut the pockets so that I can stick my hands through to use it. I open my coat just enough for the lens to peek out.

I have to take my photos secretly because I am a captive in the Lodz Ghetto. Not even the bridges go anywhere else.

I must keep on taking pictures—how else can I tell the real story of the thousands of men, women, boys, and girls trapped with me in this terrible place?

I have to wear a yellow star on my jacket because I am Jewish. The Nazis have ordered all Jews to wear these stars.

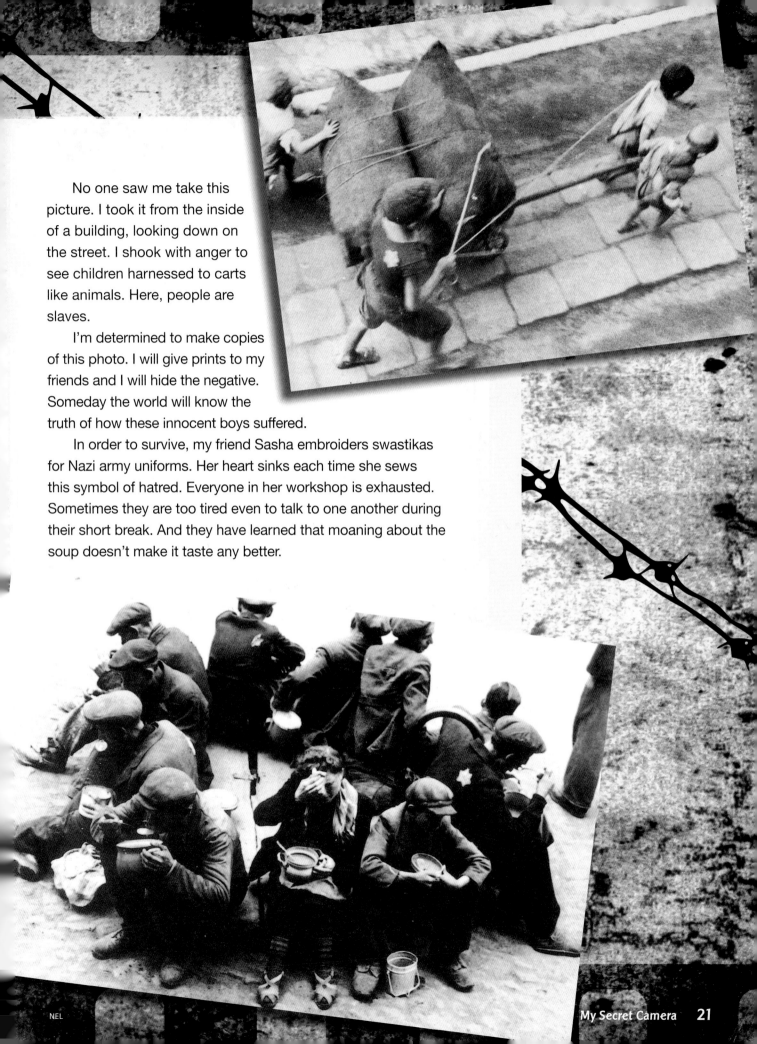

No one saw me take this picture. I took it from the inside of a building, looking down on the street. I shook with anger to see children harnessed to carts like animals. Here, people are slaves.

I'm determined to make copies of this photo. I will give prints to my friends and I will hide the negative. Someday the world will know the truth of how these innocent boys suffered.

In order to survive, my friend Sasha embroiders swastikas for Nazi army uniforms. Her heart sinks each time she sews this symbol of hatred. Everyone in her workshop is exhausted. Sometimes they are too tired even to talk to one another during their short break. And they have learned that moaning about the soup doesn't make it taste any better.

Time and time again I witness children left alone, torn from their families.

A mother to her son: "Be strong, my boy."

Just as thousands of people are forced to come into the ghetto, thousands are shipped out.

No one ever comes back.

Thousands of people pour into the ghetto every day. They come from places the Nazi army has conquered. They are confused and frightened. They have left behind everything that was familiar to them.

Reflecting

Making Inferences: What inferences about life in the Lodz Ghetto can you draw from the photos?

Metacognition: Which do you find it easier to do: make inferences while reading texts or while viewing images? Why do you think that is?

Critical Literacy: How does this photo essay affect the way you feel or think about the Holocaust? How do you think the author and photographer intended you to feel?

How to

Add Voice to Informational Writing

What tactics has this writer used to create a strong voice?

Imagine you're in hiding—in a closet or under floorboards. There's no room to blink. It's dark and dusty, too hot in summer, too cold in winter. Don't make a sound—a sneeze, a sigh, a moan. That's how thousands of children lived during the Holocaust. In hiding, anxious that they or someone else would reveal their hiding place to the Nazis. Their stories are heart-wrenching but also inspiring, because they are tales of courage, compassion, and endurance.

Take the story of Suse Grünbaum. For two years she hid with her mother in a barn, lying down in a small, coffin-like box under the floorboards in a hayloft above a pigsty.

Voice in writing is how our words sound to the reader. Writing is more enjoyable when it has a strong voice—a personality so that readers get a sense of the person behind the writing. Here are a few tactics to improve your voice and put yourself into your writing:

- Provide details and examples to back up the basic information. This will give your writing a confident voice and show that you really know your topic. When you are knowledgeable about your topic, you will sound confident and readers will pay attention.

- Show how you feel about the topic. For example, let readers know when you are curious, surprised, or worried. When you are enthusiastic, readers will hear your enthusiasm.

- Use lots of *sensory language* (words connected to sight, sound, smell, taste, touch) to paint a vivid picture.

- Compare one item or idea to another by using a simile, metaphor, or analogy. Comparisons help your audience connect with the topic.

Remember that your voice is influenced by your purpose and audience. The key to matching voice to audience is tuning in to what your readers will expect or need and how they will respond.

Transfer Your Learning

Across the Strands

Oral Communication: Think about the last speech or presentation you prepared. Which of the above tactics helped you create a strong voice?

Across the Curriculum

Geography: Which aspect of voice (knowledge or enthusiasm) would be most helpful if you were reading about a geography concept that you didn't understand? How would your choice be different if you had a good understanding of the concept?

Talk About It
Shhh! The enemy is listening!

SECRETS, LIES, AND SPIES

Article by Elizabeth MacLeod

It's a shadowy life, trading secrets and bullets, but that's the reality for many spies, knowing they may be betrayed at any time. Here are a few fascinating stories of some amazing spies who took risks simply to find and pass along secrets.

"I took my gun out of my purse. Bang. He fell down and I left."

Peggy Taylor began spying to help her mother. Peggy was born in France in 1920. World War II broke out in 1939 and when Germany invaded her country, Peggy escaped to England. Her mother was captured.

In 1942, Peggy was back in France, trained as a parachutist—and spy. Peggy soon met a German officer and passed information about him to her boss. Her boss said he'd kill the German because it was a man's job. "Well," replied Peggy, "parachuting is a man's job, too, and I've got my revolver in my handbag. I want to do it." She did. Peggy won many medals for her work. More important to Peggy, her mother survived the war. This spy moved to Canada in 1955.

He was a flying ace, inventor, millionaire, and spy.

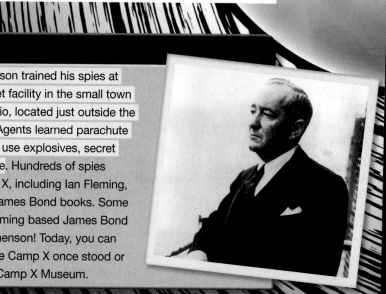

William Stephenson, the man called *Intrepid*, established Camp X, a secret training ground for spies in Canada.

William Stephenson was a flying ace, inventor, and one thing more: he was one of World War II's most important spies. He was born in Winnipeg, Manitoba, in 1896. In World War I, William shot down 20 German planes. By the time he was 30, he was a millionaire, thanks to a radio company he started in England. While living there, he became friends with British Prime Minister Winston Churchill.

In 1940, just after the start of World War II, Churchill asked William to head up a spy network based in New York City. The telegraph address of the office was Intrepid, and that became William's code name. His work included breaking codes, forging documents, exposing German spies, and protecting American factories from sabotage.

William set up the first secret agent school in North America at Camp X. There, the master spy also helped maintain Hydra, a sophisticated telecommunications centre. Messages could be coded and decoded far from the prying ears of German radio operators. Some people say William, nicknamed "The Quiet Canadian," was one of the *most* important people in the battle to defeat Adolf Hitler and the Nazis.

Voice →

Enthusiastic writers share their enthusiasm with their readers. How does this writer demonstrate her enthusiasm?

Voice →

A strong voice includes descriptive language. What does this section tell you about what Whitby was like at the time of Camp X?

Camp X

William Stephenson trained his spies at Camp X, a secret facility in the small town of Whitby, Ontario, located just outside the city of Toronto. Agents learned parachute jumping, how to use explosives, secret writing, and more. Hundreds of spies trained at Camp X, including Ian Fleming, who wrote the James Bond books. Some people claim Fleming based James Bond on William Stephenson! Today, you can visit a park where Camp X once stood or visit the nearby Camp X Museum.

This decoy spy creates havoc for German plans.

Major William Martin successfully deceived his country's enemies, although he wasn't a spy—and he never existed. In 1943, during World War II, the British planned to attack Sicily, Italy. But they wanted the Germans to think they would invade elsewhere. British Intelligence decided to "allow" the Germans to find a British officer who'd died when his plane crashed off Spain's coast. Chained to the body would be a briefcase containing details of an attack on Sardinia.

A suitable corpse was carefully dressed for its new identity as Major Martin. Then it was released from a submarine near Spain, where there were many German ships in the area. Would the Germans take the bait?

When the British received the body and briefcase back from the Germans*, the secret documents seemed unopened. However, microscopic examination showed they'd been carefully studied. When the British and their allies invaded Sicily, German troops were in Sardinia. The Allies soon took Sicily, thanks to Major Martin … the spy who never was.

*Why would the Germans return the body? you ask. Even in times of war, this was a courtesy that one country extended to another.

← **Voice**

Good writers improve their voice using a simile, metaphor, or analogy. Notice how this writer uses a metaphor here— comparing the German reaction to the spy decoy to a fish going after the bait.

Reflecting

Reading Like a Writer: If you were going to give this writer advice, what changes would you suggest to strengthen the voice? What tactics from page 24 would you suggest she focus on?

Metacognition: Which aspect of voice (knowledge or enthusiasm) do you find particularly effective in your own writing? What can you do to improve the other aspect?

Connecting to Other Media: Are the depictions of spies in this selection consistent with how spies are portrayed in other media? What spy stereotypes are you familiar with? How accurate do you think those stereotypes are?

Talk About It

What sort of difficult decisions do you think someone has to make before becoming a spy?

One Final Defiant Word

Fictionalized Letter by Su Mei Ku and Kelly Cochrane

Noor-un-nisa Inayat Khan, pictured here in her WAAF uniform

Noor-un-nisa Inayat Khan was a British spy during World War II. She was born in Moscow, Russia, in 1914 to a father who was an Indian prince and a mother from the United States. Soon after her birth, they moved to London, England, and later settled in Paris, France. This international background would serve her well as a spy.

In this selection, the authors imagine the letter Noor might have sent her nephew, David Harper, born eight years after her death. He says that he feels he knows Noor from tales his family tells. "She was a paradox. She was sensitive, a lover of music and poetry, a musician and writer of children's stories. Yet she was terribly strong-willed and prepared to risk her life for a cause."

Dear David,

Many people have asked me why I became a spy. I believed in non-violence, but how could I turn my back while the German army held France captive? Still, how could I contribute to the war, yet hold onto my beliefs?

I decided to join the Women's Auxiliary Air Force (the WAAF). They trained me to use a wireless radio to send messages. Soon the British spy organization, the Special Operations Executive (SOE), took notice of my work. The SOE needed agents to collect information behind enemy lines. I was a good candidate; I could operate a wireless radio and speak English and French.

On June 17, 1943, three other secret agents and I boarded an aircraft and were secretly flown to a meadow in northern France. From there, I was smuggled to Paris. I became known as Jeanne-Marie Regnier; my code name was Madeleine.

The mission went wrong quickly. A double agent began giving information to the Gestapo, the German secret police. Within six weeks, the Gestapo had captured almost all the SOE agents. Only a few remained free; I was one of them. I was in grave danger. The SOE repeatedly summoned me to leave Paris, but I refused. I remained in Paris, always on the run, moving from place to place to evade the Gestapo. I even hid among my enemies, staying in a building that was home to many German officers.

My luck suddenly ran out. On October 1, 1943, I returned to my apartment to find a Gestapo officer waiting for me. Someone had betrayed me. I was captured, along with my codebook. For several months after, the Germans pretended to be me, sending false information to Britain.

Every day for five weeks, the Gestapo questioned me. Each day brought increasing pressure to break my silence. I tried to escape several times. The last time I was caught and sent to a German prison. I was labelled a "very dangerous" prisoner, chained, and put in solitary confinement. The police tortured me ... I held my silence.

Nearly a year later, the Gestapo transferred three other women agents and me to Dachau, a prison camp. On the morning of September 13, 1944, we were escorted from our cells and forced to kneel in a sandy area. I stared at the guns pointed at us, and said one final, defiant word: "Liberté."

Sincerely,

Your Auntie

After the war, the British government awarded Noor the George Cross—the highest decoration for gallantry away from the battlefield. She was one of only three wartime women to receive this honour.

Reflecting

Reading Like a Writer: What aspects of voice (knowledge or enthusiasm) are strongest in this letter?

Metacognition: What ideas for your own writing do this format and treatment of a topic give you?

Critical Thinking: What can you infer about Noor's personality from this letter?

SECRET TRAINING

Informational Text by Kate Walker

students learning Japanese radio code at an American spy school during World War II

Fact File

- Most countries in the world have spy schools.
- Each of these schools trains its spies differently.

Spy Schools

Buses with Black Windows

The Central Intelligence Agency (CIA) in the United States trains its spies at Camp Peary in Virginia. It also has other, more secret training camps. One is in North Carolina. That camp has security fences and cypress trees all around. Outside is a sign that says "U.S. Navy Supply Center." No one sees the faces of the spies who come and go from this camp. They travel in buses with blacked-out windows.

The School Where Students Wore Masks

One of the most famous spy schools in the world was in the town of Baden-Baden in Germany. It operated during World War I. At this school, classes began at eight o'clock in the morning and ended late in the afternoon. Inside the school, students used **code names** and wore masks that hid the top half of their faces. Students were not allowed to make friends with other students or with people outside the school. At the end of the day, students left the school one at a time, at three-minute intervals. They were often followed to see where they went and who they talked to. While students were at the school, their apartments and belongings were searched.

British Spy Schools

In World War II, most British spies were trained in beautiful old country mansions. Today's British spies are trained on military bases, but the British will not say on which bases.

Soviet Spy Schools

During the **Cold War** (1945–1989), the **Soviet Union** spent a lot of time and money on training spies. All spies were chosen from among university students. They spent their first year learning only Soviet history and politics.

Training on the Volga

Next, students went to a special camp on the Volga River, near Kazan. This camp had guards posted at all the gates, and students were not allowed out. For a year, students learned hand-to-hand combat and how to tap phones, climb walls, and drive a wide variety of cars. Students were given tests throughout the year. To pass the course, a student had to get full marks on every test.

The Last and Most Secret Spy School

Successful students were finally sent to an ultra-secret spy camp in central Russia. The camp covered 130 km², and inside it were several different zones. There was a British zone, an American zone, a German zone, and others. Inside the American zone, for example, was a town that looked like a small North American town. Along Main Street, there were fast-food stores selling hamburgers and American newspapers. Everyone in this town spoke English with an American accent. Soviet students being trained to work in the United States spent several years in this zone. Here they learned to act and talk like Americans. It is not known if this ultra-secret camp still exists.

code names: simple names used to hide the identity of spies

Cold War: a time of distrust between the world's two superpowers, the United States and the Soviet Union, when each thought the other would attack and begin a third world war

double agent: a spy pretending to work for one country while secretly working for another

Soviet Union: a shortened name for the Union of Soviet Socialist Republics (U.S.S.R.), a large part of which has now returned to its former name, Russia.

A typical American Main Street like this one would have been part of the American zone inside the Soviets' ultra-secret spy school.

Spy Jobs

Intelligence networks have lots of people doing many different jobs. The people who work openly in intelligence offices are called the *overt staff*. What type of job might *you* get if you joined a spy agency? You might be surprised at the work you could end up doing.

Overt Staff

Backroom Boffins: Backroom boffins are scientists and builders who come up with new ideas. They make gadgets and other things that spies need.

Clerks: Clerks read foreign newspapers and other documents. When clerks find interesting information, they put it into files for the analysts.

Computer Operators: Computer operators use computers to listen in on calls between mobile phones. They search through cyberspace, read e-mails, and look for hidden messages on the Internet.

Analysts: Analysts study files of information and work out things from what they read. They write reports for the chief.

Cryptographers: Cryptographers read and write messages in secret code. They also make up code for their own agents to use. Cryptographers *crack* (solve) the codes used by other intelligence networks and read their secret messages.

Paymasters: Paymasters pay the spies. They send a great deal of money secretly to spies in different places all over the world.

The Chief: The boss of an intelligence network is called the *chief executive officer*. The chief works at network headquarters and reads reports, makes decisions, and gives orders.

Covert Staff

The people who work secretly for an intelligence network are called the *covert staff*.

Spy Master: One spy in each country is the spy master. This person sends reports to the chief and receives orders from the chief. The spy master then sends out orders to the junior spies.

Case Officers—Legal: These case officers are spies who work in foreign embassies. They recruit other agents and run several spy cells.

Mole: A mole is a special **double agent** who has managed to get into an enemy's intelligence network in a very important job. The mole pretends to work for the enemy's network but is really working against it.

Couriers: Couriers are spies who carry messages between cell leaders and case officers. Couriers do not always know what they are carrying.

Counter-Spy: A counter-spy is a double agent who has managed to get into an enemy's spy cell. The counter-spy pretends to work for the enemy's spy cell but is really working against it.

Agents of Influence: Agents of influence work on their own and report directly to the spy master.

Case Officers—Illegal: These are spies who pretend to be journalists or business people. They recruit other agents and run several spy cells.

Spy Cells: A spy cell is a group of agents. Each agent has a special skill and a different job to do. The leader of the cell is called the *cell leader*. The cell leader studies all the information gathered by the agents in the spy cell and sends reports to the case officer.

Reflecting

Reading Like a Writer: The writer has used vivid details and examples to make the voice in this piece stronger. Which details give you the best sense of what it would be like to be a spy?

Metacognition: How did using text features (such as headings, subheadings, bold text, font size, images) help you read and understand this selection?

Critical Literacy: What viewpoint or perspective on spying do you get from reading this selection? How is it the same or different from the perspective you get when watching spy movies?

How to **Make Inferences While Listening**

When you are listening to a speech, a TV show, or even your friend talking about a homework problem, you make inferences by combining what you are hearing with the way the speaker is saying it and with what you already know about the topic.

Sometimes it can be challenging to pay attention and make good inferences. Try these strategies.

☑ Make inferences to identify the speaker's perspective on the topic. How does that viewpoint compare to your own?

☑ Listen closely for new points that will add to your knowledge or change your inferences.

☑ Reflect on the speaker's tone and mood. If you hear a lot of confidence in the speaker's voice, what inferences can you make about that person's knowledge? Analyze how that confidence changes.

☑ Study the speaker's tone, body language, or facial expressions to help you make inferences while you listen.

☑ Be actively involved by taking notes, completing a graphic organizer, or asking questions.

Transfer Your Learning

Across the Strands

Media Literacy: Which of the above strategies would be most useful as you watched a TV entertainment show on the secret lives of celebrities?

Across the Curriculum

The Arts: Think of some of the songs you're currently enjoying. How frequently do you think you make inferences while listening to music? How would you assess your ability to do so?

Talk About It
How would your siblings or friends rate your ability to keep a secret?

Sibling Secrets

Making Inferences →

Identify the speaker's perspective and compare that viewpoint with your own. What do you infer about Salim's perspective on keeping secrets?

Script by Peg Kehret

Cast: Three siblings: Salim (16), Abida (15), Ghazala (14)

Setting: Minimal—any room in a family home. Need only a couple of chairs and a phone.

ABIDA: *(whispering)* Here comes Ghazala. No matter what she does, we don't hear or see her.

SALIM: This is *really* going to get to her. Especially if Jody remembers to call. Maybe it will teach her a lesson about blabbing other people's secrets.

(Ghazala enters. Abida and Salim are reading.)

GHAZALA: What are you guys doing?

SALIM: *(ignoring Ghazala)* Want to go to the library, Abida?

ABIDA: Sure, Salim.

GHAZALA: Can I go?

SALIM: Let's ride our bikes.

GHAZALA: What about *me*? Mom won't let me ride that far.

ABIDA: It's a good thing Ghazala isn't here. She'd want to tag along.

GHAZALA: *(puzzled, then growing indignant)* I *am* here. I'm standing right *next* to you.

Making Inferences

Listen closely for new points that will add to your knowledge or change your inferences. What inferences do you make as you hear more about the problem? Does that change your original inference?

SALIM: *(emphatically)* It's nice without her! We can talk without worrying she's going to eavesdrop and blab *everything* to *everyone*.

ABIDA: Our sister, the spy. *(The phone rings. Abida answers.)*

ABIDA: Hello? No, she isn't here. She isn't back from school yet.

GHAZALA: Is that for me? *(She grabs for the phone.)* Give me that. *(Salim hangs up.)*

ABIDA: Wow, that was a *boy* for Ghazala!

GHAZALA: A boy called for me, and you said I wasn't here?

SALIM: Maybe we should run next door and tell the Taylor kids that *Ghazala* got a call from a *boy*!

GHAZALA: No! Kevin Taylor will tell the whole school. *(On the verge of tears, Ghazala suddenly gasps and clutches her chest. She collapses on the floor.)*

ABIDA: *(Abida and Salim rush to her and kneel beside her.)* What's wrong? What happened? *(Ghazala is unresponsive, eyes closed.)*

ABIDA: I'm going to call 9-1-1. *(Abida grabs the phone.)*

SALIM: What if she's *pretending* she's sick to get even with us for ignoring her?

ABIDA: *(hesitates)* What if she *isn't* pretending?

SALIM: *(urgently)* Call 9-1-1. I'll do CPR. *(Salim tilts Ghazala's head back and sticks his finger in her mouth.)*

GHAZALA: *(turns her head away)* Blah. Get your hand out of my mouth! *(Abida hangs up. Salim jumps to his feet.)*

Making Inferences

Reflect on the speakers' tone and mood. What can you infer about the siblings' true feelings for Ghazala?

ABIDA: *(harshly)* You little *fake!*

GHAZALA: *Me? You've* been pretending you couldn't hear me!

SALIM: Wait till Mom finds out you faked a heart attack.

GHAZALA: If you tell Mom that, *I'll* tell her why I *had* to do it. I'll tell her everything!

ABIDA: You will anyway!

GHAZALA: *(sadly)* If you would include me once in a while, maybe I *wouldn't! (Salim and Abida look at each other surprised.)* It's *always* two against one. How do you think *I* feel? No matter where you're going, if I want to go, too, you say *no.*

SALIM: You *have* to admit, you *do* follow us around and listen to what we say.

GHAZALA: I won't repeat anything you say, ever again.

SALIM: You won't tattle to Mom and Dad?

GHAZALA: Never. *(Salim and Abida nod at one another, satisfied.)* Who called for me?

SALIM: It was Jody. We told her to call.

GHAZALA: *(Stares at them for a second, stunned. Then laughs.)* Actually, if you had done that to anyone but me, I would think it was funny.

ABIDA: Maybe she really is getting mature.

SALIM: Finally. *(They exit all together.)*

Making Inferences

The speaker's tone, body language, or facial expressions can help you make inferences. What inferences can you make about each character in this passage?

Making Inferences

Be actively involved in listening by taking notes, completing a graphic organizer, or asking questions. If you were a friend of Ghazala's and witnessed this scene, what questions would you ask her or her siblings?

Reflecting

Making Inferences: What inferences about the characters did you make? What clues in the text help you make inferences about how the characters feel?

Metacognition: How does making conscious use of strategies help you to listen effectively? When are these strategies particularly helpful to you as a student?

Critical Literacy: What aspects of this dialogue make it believable or not believable? Explain.

Talk About It

Where is your secret place?

My Secret Place

Spoken Word Poem by Michelle Muir

Spoken word poetry is a form of poetry that is intended to be performed, sometimes accompanied by music. This poetic form uses rhythm, but not necessarily rhyme, to explore a topic or express an emotion. Spoken word poetry has the same artistic roots as hip hop and rap.

When I need to be alone
In my very crowded home;
When I need to breathe
In my own personal space,
I go to the most private place I know.

This special spot I've got,
Takes me far and away
When I've had enough
Of all the stuff
I have to deal with every day.

In my space, I'm away from my brother's constant prying
And my little sister's crying.
It's the place where I can be ... free.
Free to be the me I want to be.
The me I want the world to see.
That me isn't tongue-tied
And forever trying to hide
Behind the kid who sits in front of me.

My space is my private word place
And the pen in my hand
Just seems to understand my need to write.
My pen feels so light as it slides across the page
And moves with my wrist
Like it wants to twist
The words out of me,
Like it can't wait to see
What I'm going to say next.

As far as my space goes,
I chose the most personal place in the apartment
And even though it's a small, box-looking compartment,
I can stay there for hours at a time....
Running the water to hide my tears, and my fears, and my laughter.
I am constantly adding to the list of goals I am after.

In my world of words
No idea goes unheard,
No thought gets dismissed or laughed away.
In my secret writing nook
It's just me and my notebook
And I write down all of the things
I'm not yet ready to say.

poet Michelle Muir
in her secret place

Reflecting

Making Inferences: Where is this author's secret place? What evidence in the poem supports your answer?

Metacognition: What strategies helped you make inferences about this selection?

Critical Thinking: Have you ever felt as Michelle feels in the following lines? What do you think she means?

> **In my secret writing nook**
> **It's just me and my notebook**
> **And I write down all of the things**
> **I'm not yet ready to say.**

How to # Create a Comic

Making a graphic comic can be fun. Just like creating other media texts though, it does help to start by examining lots of good examples. Learn about the different styles and conventions first. Then follow these steps to create your own graphic comic.

My Big Idea: short mystery story about the secret ingredients in the cafeteria's chili con carne
Best Style: mysterious, menacing, ominous, black and white images

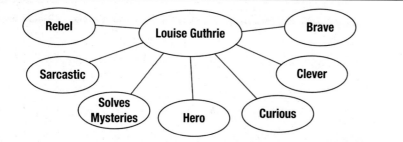

◄ **Step 1: Decide what your story will be about.**

What's your big idea or theme? Think about how long your comic will be and the style that fits your theme. For example, superhero comics often use colourful, flashy art; funny comics use simple black and white line art and exaggerated expressions.

◄ **Step 2: Create an outline and a character web for your main character.**

How many characters will you need? What will happen to them? What's your setting? Start thinking about how each event will be developed in one or more frames.

◄ **Step 3: Experiment with drawing your characters.**

What should your characters look like? Draw rough sketches of your characters in different situations and with different expressions.

Step 4: Create a first draft layout showing every frame with rough sketches and speech bubbles.

Not all frames have to be the same size or shape. Small frames can help you create a faster pace while larger frames emphasize important scenes. Use a variety of angles and distances in each frame. Close-ups can show tension or emotion while full-figure shots can show action.

You may want to show this draft to a few people to get their feedback.

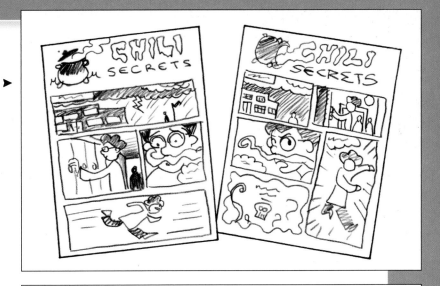

Step 5: Create a final draft.

In each panel, word balloons should be read from left to right, top to bottom, like a regular story. Write the dialogue first and then draw the balloon to fit the words. Don't try to make the words fit into a balloon that's too big or too small.

Step 6: Print your dialogue neatly in your speech bubbles.

Now you're ready to draw your characters and setting around the balloons. Use pencil or ink. Using dark lines or shapes can make your comic more moody. Action lines can add excitement and tension. You may want to add colour.

Transfer Your Learning

Across the Strands

Writing: When performing a complicated task, having clear guidelines to follow can make the task easier. What aspects of creating a graphic comic could help you with your writing?

Across the Curriculum

History: What story from your history text do you think would best be told using a graphic comic? What style of comic would you use?

Talk About It
What's the hardest part about keeping a secret?

GHAZALA'S SECRET

Creating a Comic →

Comic by Daniel Lafrance and Andy Belanger

The first step in creating a comic is deciding what the story will be about. Read the title and skim these images. What story are these artists going to tell?

Creating a Comic →

Then create an outline and character web, and experiment with drawing the characters. As you read this comic, think about the story and character decisions the artists made. Would you have made similar decisions?

Creating a Comic

An important step is to create a first draft to plan every frame. Think about the decisions these artists made about the size of frames or the perspectives in the frames.

← Creating a Comic

The last step in developing a comic is creating the final draft by drawing figures and objects carefully, printing dialogue neatly, and, possibly, adding colour. How successfully have the artists told their story?

Reflecting

Creating Media Texts: Think of another selection in this unit that you enjoyed. How would you represent that selection—from the same or a different perspective—using a comic? List some of the decisions you would make to create that comic.

Metacognition: How does analyzing a comic help you understand how to create one? What else do you need to help you understand the process?

Critical Literacy: What stereotypes do the artists depend on to help their readers understand the characters and the situation?

Talk About It

There's an old folk tale that compares the spread of gossip to feathers blowing in the wind—they spread everywhere, and you can never gather them all up again.

Word Gets Around ...

Comic by Catherine Rondina and Dan Workman

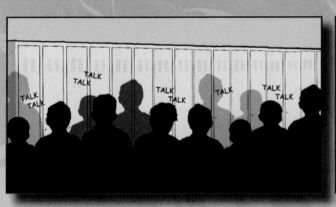

Reflecting

Creating Comics: How does the depiction of these characters contribute to the author's message?

Metacognition: How does examining comic strips help you learn about creating them?

Critical Literacy: What stereotype does this selection use? How do you respond to that stereotype?

Generalization

Generalization text pattern organizes information by beginning with a general statement followed by facts, reasons, or examples that support the statement. You often see this pattern when a writer wants to present an argument. The writer will make a statement, and then make points to support that statement. Sometimes the writer will also present the opposing points, and then argue against them.

The quality of the argument and the organization of the text work together to create a strong piece. Writers who use this text pattern effectively follow these guidelines:

- State their viewpoint clearly, often in the topic sentence of the first paragraph.
- Check that the points supporting their argument are from a trustworthy source (such as experts, books, newspapers, or reliable Internet sites). Make sure they cite the source.
- Consider opposing viewpoints fairly, and use logical arguments to counter those viewpoints.

Generalization

Viewpoint — Opposing Viewpoint

Support — Support — Logical Argument — Logical Argument

Transfer Your Learning

Across the Strands

Oral Communication: You could use generalization text pattern in a presentation or speech. What topic are you studying now that would benefit from using this pattern?

Across the Curriculum

Geography: Provide support for the following generalization: Levels of education are one of the best indicators of a country's wealth.

Talk About It
What secrets does your handwriting reveal?

The Writing's on the Wall

The Dark Secrets Revealed by Every Word We Write
Informational Article by Janice Dineen

Generalization
Text Pattern

Selections using generalization text pattern begin with a generalization that will be supported with subsequent information. What generalization is made here? As you continue to read, think about how this generalization is supported.

Generalization
Text Pattern

Selections using generalization text pattern may use key words that can help you analyze the argument. What word in this section indicates generalization text pattern? How does that word help you analyze the generalization?

Handwriting is used to help catch thieves, spies, and murderers. But even if you don't have a criminal bent, your handwriting can say a lot about you. Do you write your letter *Y* with a little open curl at the bottom, the one handwriting analysts call "the felon's claw"? It's a writing trait you share with 80 percent of convicted criminals.

Do you make wide loops in the stems of your *T*s and small *D*s? A *graphologist* (handwriting expert) would suspect you are terribly sensitive to criticism. Perhaps you form your letter *E* in the Greek way, with one semi-circle on top of another. That may show your literary talent and creative tendencies.

People who study the subject argue that your handwriting reveals a vast amount of information about you: your strengths and weaknesses, your lifestyle, your level of honesty, and your habits.

Handwriting Analysis Solves the Case

When three houses being guarded by an American security company were broken into in six months, the firm hired handwriting analyst Andrea McNichol to examine samples of handwriting from several of its employees. Andrea asked the employees to write about what they were doing during the time the third house was robbed.

1. Who is the felon, A or B?

A.

I am

B.

I am

The answer is A, who writes with a "felon's claw," a curved hook coming off a straight down stroke. Over 80 percent of convicted felons write with this claw shape.

In the sample provided by one man, she noticed a curious change of slant when he wrote certain words denying he was anywhere in the area of the burglary at the time. Andrea alerted the head of the company, who kept an eye on the man. A few months later, he was caught breaking into another house.

Study of Handwriting: A Wonderful Tool

Your handwriting, Andrea says, is an X-ray of your mind. "We should really call it *brain-writing* because it doesn't come from your hand. It's a wonderful, wonderful tool. No two people on Earth have ever had exactly the same handwriting."

The study of handwriting is as old as writing itself. Aristotle (an ancient Greek philosopher) was interested in it. When someone was doing cave drawings, there was probably another cave person right behind analyzing the style.

Worldwide Reliance on Handwriting Analysis

Today, handwriting analysis is widely used by employers in Europe to assess employees and job applicants. Some North American corporations use it and many law enforcement agencies do also.

"I've trained FBI agents and police officers of all kinds," observes Andrea, who was hired as an FBI expert in the case of the disputed handwritten Howard Hughes will. Pinpointing the will as a fraud was a snap, she says. It was dated at a time when Howard had an illness that caused his hands to shake. The will was written by a steady hand.

Generalization Text Pattern →

Consider whether other generalizations are made. What further generalizations are suggested in this paragraph? Are they supported? How do they support the main generalization?

Generalization Text Pattern →

Good writers use supporting points from a trustworthy source. What makes Andrea McNichol a reliable source?

Revealing the Secrets in Handwriting

Andrea claims that the study of handwriting gives insight into a person's personality. Here are some of the handwriting theories she teaches in her handwriting analysis course at UCLA:

- A left slant shows someone who holds feelings back. A right slant shows someone who expresses emotions more easily. An extreme right slant shows emotions out of control.

- Writing with heavy pressure indicates vitality, mental intensity, assertiveness, or frustration. Light pressure suggests illness, tiredness, intoxication, or spirituality.

- An uneven left margin on the page suggests a writer who dislikes discipline and can't stick to the rules. Someone who leaves no margins at the left or right won't recognize other people's rights and opinions.

- Open ovals show frankness or a talkative tendency. Loops in the ovals indicate a secretive nature. Little stabbing marks into the ovals suggest chronic lying.

Handwriting Analysis a Matter of Common Sense

Much of handwriting analysis is based on common sense, Andrea argues. You can figure out that someone with large handwriting is more extroverted and people-oriented, and someone with tiny, cramped writing is more introverted and task-oriented.

But she and other graphologists have refined it all to an incredible level of detail. They read the strength of your work drive in the length and strength of the line you use to cross your *T*. They decide you are generous because you finish your words with a big, swirling end stroke.

2. Who would make a better salesperson, A or B?

A. *who would make the better salesman?*

B. *I would like to go into sales. I think I could be very good.*

The answer is A. Large writing indicates an extrovert who wants to go out into his or her environment, a good trait for a salesperson. Small writing indicates introversion and self-involvement.

3. Who is more "crooked," A or B?

A. *who is more crooked do you think?*

B. *who is more crooked do you think*

The answer is B, whose writing is wedged like bent teeth on a saw blade. That indicates someone who is dangerously dishonest, criminalistic, and crooked—like the writing.

And they have compared so many samples of handwriting from prison inmates with samples from the general public that they have identified 18 writing characteristics they believe suggest dishonesty. Such writing traits as a lot of retracing, letters broken into segments, or forming the letters *a* and *o* just like each other, are a few suspicious signs.

Andrea says a sample of your handwriting gives away more about you than a lie detector test. She claims she can see who is violent versus who is merely devious, and who has planned a crime versus who has done it spontaneously, just by looking at handwriting samples.

Does your handwriting look as if a chicken walked across the page? Messy writing isn't necessarily a bad sign, graphologists say. If it is totally illegible to anyone else, it may mean that you're not interested in communicating with others, or that you have a certain thoughtless abandon in your nature.

But overly precise, perfectly formed letters flowing in a highly controlled way in exactly straight lines is much more worrying, according to Andrea. This is the writing of someone so repressed that Andrea would conclude the person is dangerous.

Change Your Handwriting— Change Yourself?

Someone with very tidy, conventional writing is likely to be a conventional person, says Elaine Charal, a Toronto graphologist whose Don Mills firm is called Positive Strokes. "Your writing is like a paper mirror," she says. "You'll see your writing change as the experiences of your life change you. Your slant can shift three or four times a day, depending on your mood."

When Elaine first had her own handwriting analyzed almost 20 years ago, the graphologist told her she had a tendency to be clingy, but she could do handwriting exercises called *graphotherapy* to help her change. She worked on it and noticed a difference over time. "You can't change your T-bars and become a perfect person," Elaine says. "You have to change your behaviours with your handwriting, but the changes can come hand in hand."

Handwriting is such a potent reflection of your personal characteristics, Elaine says, that people who lose the use of one hand and end up writing with the other, or people who lose the use of both hands and end up writing with their mouth, have the same basic characteristics reflected in their writing no matter what they write with.

Elaine says that pointed *N*s and *M*s indicate someone who is quick thinking. A straight, stick-like stem on the letters *Y* and *Q* suggests someone who is a bit of a loner, and who may prefer to work on his/her own authority.

A signature smaller than the rest of the writing can show that the writer is feeling diminished. If the last letters in your words continue to flow into a line or swoop, it reflects what a generous person you are. Dotting your *i*'s with a little circle indicates a desire for attention.

Elaine says there are few qualified people doing handwriting analysis in Canada. But qualifications aren't always clear-cut in the field. There are no formal educational credentials and no licensing or regulation.

← **Generalization Text Pattern**

Good writers consider opposing viewpoints fairly. What information in this paragraph cautions the reader about the original generalization in this selection?

Reflecting

Analyzing Text Pattern: Does the support provided convince you that the generalization is correct? If not, what other support do you think is required?

Metacognition: How does knowing the characteristics of generalization text pattern help you understand this selection?

Critical Literacy: What questions does this selection not raise about the information it includes? In your opinion, what points or arguments should have been considered?

SECRETS
NECESSARY AND DANGEROUS

Essay by Kathy Evans

Knowing a secret can be deliciously exciting; it can give our lives drama and a sense of power. But keeping a secret takes effort. The weight of it can feel like a burden, to be lifted only when the secret is told. And telling a secret can lead to hurt and distrust. You'll know this if you've ever told a friend's secret.

We all have secrets. From the bully in the schoolyard to the leader in the highest political office, we all have secrets. Secrets are everywhere. Little secrets about the chocolate bar you pinched from your brother. Big secrets about government conspiracies.

One theory about secrecy, then, is that it is both necessary and dangerous. One expert says, "Secrecy is as indispensable to human beings as fire, and as greatly feared."

If you doubt the above opinion, just think about all the secrets you're keeping. How difficult is it for you to know when to keep a secret and when to tell someone you trust? If you answered, "Very difficult," you're not alone.

Secrecy and Security

Most of the secrets we keep are for our personal protection. This type of secrecy is closely related to privacy and security—secrecy as safety. For example, we know it's not wise to share personal information, such as a computer password. Most of us have a secret and private place where we stash our valuable possessions or our personal mementoes and treasures. Have you ever hidden away something precious so a younger brother or sister didn't break it? It's human nature to keep parts of our lives hidden, but many of these examples show that secrecy is also necessary for our own protection.

Government Secrets

Governments are good at keeping secrets. Lots of them. Too many, some people would say. One reason that is frequently given is national security. Countries don't want other countries to know their military secrets. After all, how effective can a special secret force be if its operations aren't secret?

Governments have vast amounts of information. Maybe the best we can do is to be aware that governments mostly choose what information they want to share with us. In a 2002 report, Canada's Information Commissioner wrote, "Once again we are ... confronted with the reality that bureaucrats like secrets—they always have; they will go to absurd lengths to keep secrets from the public and even from each other."

Secrets in Business

Competition in business is tough, and being unique is often a company's best hope for success. As a result, corporations have secrets. The recipe for Kentucky Fried Chicken. The Spring collection of a famous clothing designer. A new drug for high blood pressure. Ford's plans for the next Mustang model. The design for the next version of iPod. Some companies have strict privacy polices, or confidentiality agreements, that make sure employees don't leak company information. This type of secrecy is necessary for businesses to stay a step ahead of the competition and avoid being copied. Generally, employees and the public understand and accept this kind of corporate secrecy. Just like you keep your incredible science project idea secret from the rest of your class until you have to reveal it. You don't want anyone to steal your idea.

But what would you do if you were an employee and discovered a company secret that you knew was wrong? Cynthia Cooper knew what to do. In 2002, she detected and exposed fraud within her company, the largest corporate fraud in U.S. history. The chief financial officer was fired, and the company went bankrupt.

Another employee who went public with damaging information is Jeffrey Wigand. In the 1990s, he revealed some dark secrets about his company and the U.S. tobacco industry. He reported that consumers were misled about the addictiveness of nicotine and other dangers of tobacco products.

People like Cynthia Cooper and Jeffrey Wigand are often called *whistleblowers*; they uncover secrets and expose wrongdoing. Standing up to a corporation or industry is not easy—many people who have gone public with information end up losing their jobs and are not hired by other firms.

Many people fear disclosing damaging information about the company they work for. But some people take that brave and lonely step to disclosure. Because, as Martin Luther King, Jr., said, "Our lives begin to end the day we become silent about things that matter." For example, would you remain silent if you saw someone you knew dumping old tires or other garbage into a nearby stream?

What do these examples show about secrecy and business? When companies try to veil wrongdoing in misinformation and cover-ups, that's when secrecy can be dangerous. That's when the public needs the truth.

Conclusions

Secrecy is a part of life. Most secrets are practical and of no serious consequence. Secrets can even be intriguing and exciting. Secrecy does carry a more menacing element. How do we handle that dangerous side of secrecy? As for secrecy for self-protection, it's probably wise to always ask yourself if you're getting the whole story or the true story. What could happen if you don't get the whole or true story? Sorry, that's classified.

Reflecting

Analyzing Text Pattern: What does the author do in this selection that helps you recognize it as generalization text pattern?

Metacognition: How does your understanding of the text pattern help you to weigh the credibility of this article?

Media Literacy: What movies have you seen in which a secret was an important part of the story line? What different attitudes to the secret did different characters have?

The reading strategy you learned in this unit can help you better understand text in other subject areas. As you read this science text, look for clues to help you make inferences.

Technological Advances of the Microscope

Revealing the Secrets in Cells

Advances in cell biology are directly linked to advances in optics. As biologists see and learn more about cells, they want instruments that provide them with greater detail. Optical scientists and technologists respond by investigating light, and by creating better and better light microscopes. More recent advances in technology have produced powerful microscopes that allow biologists to see more detail and develop a deeper understanding of the functions of the cells that make up organisms.

FIGURE 1

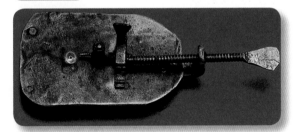

(a) Anton Van Leeuwenhoek's microscopes used a single lens mounted between two brass plates to magnify objects.

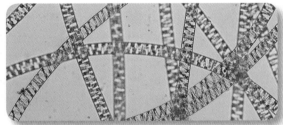

(b) Algae viewed at 10X magnification. Some algae are single-celled organisms.

The Single-Lens Microscope

Some of the best early microscopes were made in the 1660s by Anton Van Leeuwenhoek. He was curious about the microscopic world and constantly worked at improving his design. His microscope (Figure 1) had only a single lens and acted like a simple magnifying glass. It magnified things 10 or more times (usually written as *10X*, where *X* means "times"). Anton was astonished when he looked at a water drop and saw numerous tiny organisms.

The Compound Light Microscope

Biologists found a single lens limiting; they could not see the details needed to understand how cells work. An important advance came when a second lens was added to the microscope. An image magnified 10X by the first lens and 10X by the second lens is viewed as 100X larger.

There is a limit to what can be done with glass lenses and light, however. To make images larger, lenses must become thicker. As lenses become thicker, however, the images they produce begin to blur. Eventually, the image is so blurred that no detail can be seen.

The light microscope (Figure 2) is limited to about 2000X magnification. To see the detail within a human cell, greater magnification is needed. The development of the electron microscope made this possible.

The Transmission Electron Microscope

Transmission electron microscopes (Figure 3) are capable of 2 000 000X magnification! Instead of light, they use a beam of electrons that pass through the specimen of cells or tissues. (Electrons are tiny particles with a negative charge that travel around the nucleus of an atom.) The first practical electron microscope was built by physics professor Eli Franklin Burton and three of his students, in 1938 at the University of Toronto. It was only capable of 7000X magnification.

FIGURE 2

(a) light microscope

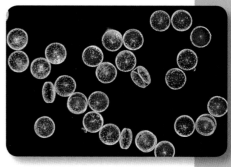

(b) algae cells seen through a light microscope

FIGURE 3

(a) The transmission electron microscope uses magnets to concentrate a beam of electrons and direct it at a specimen.

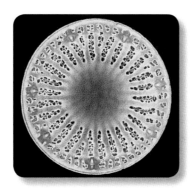

(b) alga cell section seen through a transmission electron microscope

Unfortunately, transmission electron microscopes have two major limitations. First, specimens that contain many layers of cells, such as a blood vessel, cannot be examined. The electrons are easily deflected or absorbed by a thick specimen. Very thin slices of cells (sections) must be used. These thin sections are obtained by encasing a specimen in plastic, and then shaving very thin layers off the plastic. The second limitation is that preparing cells for viewing kills them. This means that only dead cells can be observed. Although the transmission electron microscope is ideal for examining structures within a cell, it does not allow you to examine the surface details of a many-celled insect eye, or a living cell as it divides.

The Scanning Electron Microscope

The scanning electron microscope (Figure 4) was developed in response to the limitations of the transmission electron microscope. It uses electrons that are reflected off a specimen. This allows a digital, three-dimensional image to be created. Because the scanning electron microscope uses only reflected electrons, the thickness of the specimen does not matter. However, only the outside of the specimen can be seen. Also, the scanning electron microscope, capable of only 250 000X magnification, cannot magnify as much as the transmission electron microscope.

FIGURE 4

(a) scanning electron microscope

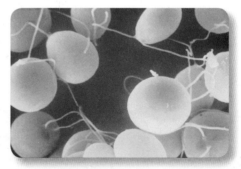

(b) algae cells seen through a scanning electron microscope

Reflecting

Making Inferences: How do words like *however*, *unfortunately*, and *though*, help you make inferences about the author's viewpoint?

Metacognition: How does using prior knowledge help you make inferences as you read this science text?

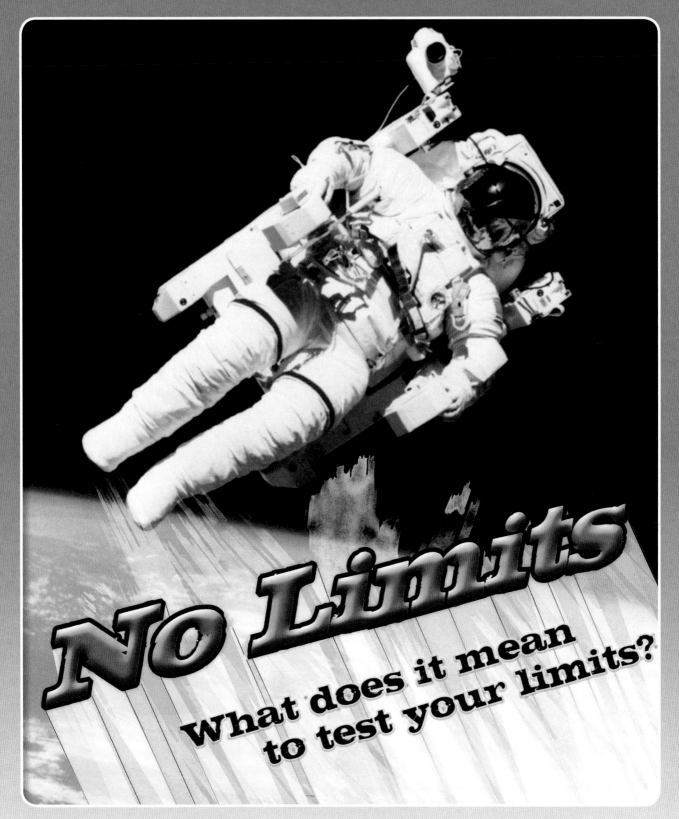

Unit Learning Goals

- summarize important ideas while reading
- improve word choice while writing
- improve understanding while listening
- identify point of view in media texts
- analyze nonfiction recount text pattern

Transfer Your Learning: Health

How to ▶ Summarize

When you create a summary for a selection, you reduce the text to its main ideas. Summarizing is a good strategy to help you understand the author's message and the ideas that support that message. Summarizing can help you study, since it helps you focus on and remember important information.

To summarize a text

☑ After you've read the whole text, identify the author's message—the main idea of the whole text. Text features, such as the title, topic sentence, or photos, can help you.

☑ Go back over each paragraph or section to identify the key ideas that support the main idea. Headings can help you. Identify the details that are essential, not just interesting.

☑ Create a summary of the text using your own words. A graphic organizer can help you identify and organize the main and key ideas. A few of the graphic organizers you might use are shown on this page. Choose one that is appropriate for the text pattern of the selection.

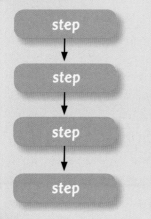

Sequence Text Pattern

As you summarize a text that uses sequence text pattern, ask yourself: What is described? What are the steps or events?

step
↓
step
↓
step
↓
step

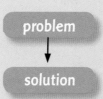

Problem/Solution Text Pattern

problem
↓
solution

As you summarize a text that uses problem/solution text pattern, ask yourself: What is the problem? What solutions are proposed?

Generalization Text Pattern

As you summarize a text that uses generalization text pattern, ask yourself: What is the main idea or opinion? What points support that idea?

generalization

supporting point

supporting point

supporting point

Transfer Your Learning

Across the Strands

Writing: How does what you've just learned relate to what you learned about organizing ideas in Unit 2 of *Nelson Literacy 8*?

Across the Curriculum

Health: If you were reading an article called "The Ten Most Important Steps to a Healthy Lifestyle," what type of graphic organizer could help you organize your summary?

Embracing the Unknown

Personal Essay by Ananda Fulton

Summarizing

When you create a summary for a selection, you reduce the text to its main ideas. From the title and first paragraph, what do you think will be the main idea of this selection? What evidence in the text supports your answer?

It's easier to continue in old habits than to try something new, which might not work out well. Trying something new means taking a risk: taking a risk that you might fail, that people might criticize you, or that you might really dislike whatever you try. However, trying something new also means accepting a challenge, embracing the unknown, and having the chance to discover things you never knew about the world or about yourself.

I wasn't someone who takes a lot of risks. I was never much for trying a new activity or game (what if I was bad at it?), or going to new places (what if I didn't like the new place, or worse, the people there didn't like me?). I also avoided speaking in front of people, because there was always the risk that I might say something weird, or look weird, or forget my speech. I was afraid to accept new challenges for fear I might fail. I stuck with what I knew and avoided the unknown.

What, Me Audition?

Then, in my first year of high school, a friend of mine asked me to audition for a part in a school play with him. Of course I said, "No way!" Auditioning for a play involved all the things I avoided: taking a risk, doing something new, and talking in front of people! My friend was pretty convincing though. He told me all about the play, and said that no one would judge me if I wasn't good in my audition, they would think it was cool that I came out and gave it a shot. I was nervous, but I agreed to audition because I realized I really wanted to try acting.

Summarizing

Text features, such as title, topic sentences, and headings, can help you identify the author's message. At this point, what do you think the author's message is? As you continue reading, keep that message in mind and consider how it is developed or supported.

Dead   Deadstock

I got the script for the play, read it, and then decided on the part that I wanted to play. It was the part of this mischievous girl who goes around town playing well-meaning tricks on people that make them realize the mistakes they're making in their lives. She was a clever, funny, gutsy character, and I thought that was the kind of person I would like to play just for a while.

A Huge Risk with a Big Payoff

As the date of the audition got closer and closer, I got more and more nervous. It seemed like a huge risk to get up on stage in front of people and try to convince them I could act. What if I was so nervous that my hands shook, or I tripped, or I forgot the lines? What if they laughed? To calm myself down, I practised the lines for my audition in the mirror every day and memorized them completely.

On the day of the audition I almost backed out. It would have been easy. No one knew I was going to audition except my friend, and he would have understood. I felt that it was going to be too hard, that it wasn't worth the stress, and what would being in a play do for me anyway. Then I realized that it was a challenge, a risk, and even if I didn't succeed in getting the part, I could feel good about accepting that challenge. So, I went into the auditorium, I climbed the steps to the stage, and I delivered my lines as if I was just as gutsy as my character. Afterward, I felt excited, and I was proud of myself. It was a new feeling. It's hard to be proud of yourself when you're always doing the same old things that you already know how to do. On audition day, I felt that I had done something different, something difficult, and that I had succeeded, whether I got the part or not.

As it turned out, I did get the part, my friend got a part, too, and being in the play was a blast! I met the rest of the actors, mostly high-school seniors, and even though they didn't know me, they embraced me and became my friends. We worked very hard, staying for hours after school, and having rehearsals on the weekends. I didn't know I could work that hard. I learned that I had talents I didn't even know about, and I learned that there are a whole lot more people who work on a play than just the actors on stage.

Summarizing →

Reread each paragraph or section to help you identify key ideas that support the author's message. What details in this paragraph support the author's message?

Discovering Yourself

After months of hilarious, exhausting, and exhilarating rehearsals, we performed the play at the school. Then, we went to a festival, which is like a competition for plays, and performed there. We won an award, which meant that we went to an even bigger festival. At these festivals I met more people I didn't know, and I discovered that it's exciting to meet new people and learn about how they got to the festival and where they're from. Doing something new wasn't nearly as scary as I thought it would be. We were all people who had taken a risk, worked hard, and succeeded in doing something challenging.

If I could go back in time to visit my younger self, I would tell her to take risks and to always welcome a challenge. When you work hard for something you want, you can feel proud no matter what the outcome, and you'll probably succeed a lot more than you might think! Remember, you can't succeed if you don't try. Best of all, when you try something new you open yourself up to possibilities and to learning more about yourself. Discovering more about who you really are and what you are capable of will help you in every aspect of life. You will have the knowledge to choose your own goals and the confidence to take on all challenges along the way.

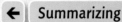

Summarizing

Create a summary of the text using your own words. For this selection, start by stating the author's purpose. Identify the key ideas in each paragraph. Thinking about how the text is organized can help you.

Reflecting

Summarizing: Identifying the author's purpose can help you identify the text pattern, and knowing the text pattern can help you summarize. What is this author's purpose? What is the text pattern of the selection? Which graphic organizer from page 62 would you use to summarize this selection?

Metacognition: How does knowing the text structure help you summarize and make meaning of the text? What else do you do to help you summarize a text?

Critical Literacy: Do you agree with this author's message? Why or why not? Think about how other people might respond to this text.

AGAINST GREAT ODDS

Emily Jennings Stowe—Becoming the First Canadian Female Physician

Nonfiction Recount by Tanya Lloyd Kyi

Emily Jennings Stowe

Emily Jennings Stowe and Jennie Trout stepped into the lecture hall, heads held high. They were the first women ever to attend the University of Toronto's medical classes and the male students and professors found new ways each week to shock or embarrass them, hoping the women would quit. But for Emily and Jennie, this was the battle of a lifetime. There was no way they would give up.

Still, that day they had to stifle a scream when they saw their seats. Someone had taken the hands from a *cadaver* (a body used for medical research) and placed them on the women's chairs. When Emily gasped, the lecture hall roared with laughter. Glaring, she gingerly lifted the hand from her seat and sat down. Jennie did the same.

Emily was born in 1831 in what is now Ontario. She was raised by her parents, former Mennonites, to believe that men and women were equal—a startling belief for the times. By the time she was 15, Emily was teaching in the local Norwich school. In search of further education, she applied to the University of Toronto. She was turned down. The school didn't allow female students.

Jennie Trout

Undefeated, Emily attended teacher's college and, by age 20, she was the principal of Brantford's public school and the first female principal in Canada.

In 1856, at age 25, Emily married a carriage maker named John Stowe. In many school boards, married women were not allowed to teach, so Emily gave up her job to care for John and the three children that soon arrived. But when John caught tuberculosis and grew too sick to work, something had to be done. Emily found work at a nearby private school that was less strict about married women teaching. Still, she earned half the wages of the male teachers.

Frustrated by her treatment at the school and bored with her classes, Emily made a bold decision. Returning home one day, she announced to her family that she was going to medical school. Saving every spare penny for tuition, she applied to the University of Toronto, which again turned her down. There were still no women allowed.

Recruiting her sister to care for the children, Emily travelled to the United States to attend the New York Medical College for Women. She graduated in 1867 and when she opened her clinic in Toronto, she became the first Canadian woman to practise medicine in Canada.

Emily's clinic was always busy. Tired of the poor treatment they received from some male doctors, and more comfortable with a woman, patients flocked to Emily's examining room. But a new law in Canada required all doctors trained in the United States to complete at least one semester of classes at a Canadian medical school and to write Canadian medical exams. Unfortunately for Emily, no Canadian medical school would admit female students.

Her choices were to give up her practice or continue without a medical licence. Emily refused to give up. She was fined. She was threatened with prison time. The Ontario College of Physicians and Surgeons stood against her. Emily's clinic remained open illegally for 13 years.

Finally, Emily and one other woman, Jennie Trout, were allowed to attend a semester of classes at the University of Toronto, on one condition. They were not allowed to complain. In classes, they met more harassment than ever before. Students left obscene messages on the blackboards before class. Professors gave lewd lectures designed to embarrass them.

After one particularly disgusting lecture, Emily marched up to the professor. "Doctor," she said firmly, "if you continue to lecture in this way, I will be repeating every word of what you say to your wife." That professor didn't bother the women again, and Emily and Jennie continued to ignore the students' taunts until they both successfully finished the term. Emily was finally granted a licence to practise medicine in 1880.

But her fight wasn't over. Angered by the powerlessness of the women she treated, she started the Toronto Women's Suffrage Club, a group that fought for women's rights. They campaigned for improved working conditions and wages, they lobbied the universities to admit women, and they demanded the right to vote.

Some of their campaigns were successful. In 1883, Emily's daughter Augusta became the first woman to receive a medical degree in Canada. She went on to teach at the newly formed Women's Medical College in Ontario.

Emily Stowe died in 1903.

Due to the continuing work of women's rights groups, women won the right to vote in Ontario in 1917.

Fast Fact

In 1896, Emily and her daughter acted in a mock parliament. Pretending to be members of government, the women debated whether men should be granted the right to vote. After all, if men were voting, who would care for the children? The mock parliament won acclaim in the press and embarrassed the government.

Reflecting

Summarizing: What was this author's purpose? Which of the organizers provided on page 62 would you use to help you summarize this selection? Why?

Metacognition: How did you determine which organizer was most appropriate for summarizing this selection?

Critical Literacy Thinking: How do you think a man or woman from the time period of this text would react to its tone?

Talk About It
What do you know about the *fight or flight response*?

ADRENALIN
YOUR BODY IN GEAR

Informational Article by Meghan Newton

What Is Adrenalin?

Adrenalin is a natural chemical in your body—it provides the "rush" feeling you get when you parachute out of a plane, perform in front of an audience, or when you face a new challenge. Adrenalin is also released throughout a typical day. Both good stress (such as the excitement you feel when talking about your weekend plans) and bad stress (such as the nervousness you feel when you have to give a presentation) can trigger the release of adrenalin. Adrenalin helps you focus and concentrate on tasks.

What Happens During an Adrenalin Rush?

When an adrenalin rush develops in the body, two hormones (adrenalin and cortisol) are released from the adrenal glands that sit on top of the kidneys. These hormones speed everything up, putting your body in high-performance mode. This bodily response is hard-wired into human brains; it is called the *fight or flight response* because your body is now primed to fight the threat or run away fast! But you have more options than just fighting or running: you can perform everyday tasks—such as talking, eating, and thinking—more quickly. With the help of adrenalin, you can get a lot done.

Here's what happens in your body during an adrenalin rush:

- You start to breathe faster. This is your body trying to get more oxygen into the lungs. The more oxygen in the lungs, the more oxygenated blood the heart can pump to the muscles.

- Your body wants to pump blood faster, too; the more oxygen in the blood, the heavier it is, and the harder and faster the heart pumps to get blood flowing to the muscles.

- Your senses are heightened—you're on the alert, ready for action.

- When you're first injured, say in an accident, the body's perception of pain is deadened. This is why many people experience no pain at first and can walk on injured limbs.

- Blood is also diverted from other areas to the muscles and limbs to give them the fuel and energy to move fast.

- As well, the liver drops sugar into the blood for your muscles to use.

Side Effects

However, if you're sitting on the couch watching TV (and not running away from a sabre-toothed tiger), the sugar released by adrenalin doesn't get used. Your body tries to correct this imbalance by releasing *insulin* (a hormone that helps your body control blood sugar), but often your liver releases too much insulin. Insulin attacks sugar so ferociously that the body must then protect other body parts from the insulin. It does this by coating the arteries with cholesterol.

Side Effects Flow Chart

stress triggers adrenalin

↓

that causes sugar dump

↓

that causes release of insulin

↓

that can increase cholesterol

↓

that can lead to high cholesterol

Running on Empty

The amount of adrenalin in each person varies, but the body has a limited amount that can be used in a 24-hour period. Once these stores are depleted, the body is no longer able to go into fight or flight response mode. Instead of feeling energized, you feel exhausted, ready to crash and burn.

People can experience adrenalin crashes after a busy day at school or work, at the end of a big project, or at the beginning of a vacation when they have "nothing to do."

As well, once you crash, you may get sick. The reason: high adrenalin boosts your immune system. When you come down off an extended adrenalin high, your immune system is lowered. Adrenalin also makes the body forget hunger, but once the adrenalin rush is over, your body will have no fuel to run on: you're burnt out. Time to gear down, relax, and refuel.

Reflecting

Summarizing: What is the main message of this selection? What key points support that message?

Metacognition: How does summarizing the selection help you remember important information? How does making connections help you understand the information?

Critical Literacy: Has the editor of this article chosen images, colours, and font styles that are appropriate for the content and tone of the text? Support your answer.

ONE OF A KIND

Basketball MVP Steve Nash

Profile by Jeff Rud from *Steve Nash: The Making of an MVP*

Canadian Steve Nash is point guard for the Phoenix Suns of the National Basketball Association. He was voted most valuable player for the league two seasons running, in 2004–2005 and 2005–2006. He is ranked as one of the top players in the league's history on many fronts, including: three-point shooting, free throws, total assists, and assists per game. Steve is also heavily involved in charity and humanitarian work. In December 2007, it was announced that he would receive Canada's highest civilian honour, the Order of Canada.

Steve Nash: not exactly your average NBA superstar. There is not much that is average about Steve, athletically or otherwise.

Steve was a standout basketball player in high school, as the vast majority of his NBA counterparts were. However, few of them played just one season of high-school ball, hailed from the hoops hinterland of Canada, or had to sweat it out to see whether they'd get even a single college scholarship offer.

"I always felt like I could get there," Steve says now of his unusual path to the peak of the basketball world. "I always felt like I could improve, and I think there were many times that built on top of each other—where you realized you can do it, you can keep improving. You can't really pick one as the turning point, but there are a lot of moments that add to your belief and confidence."

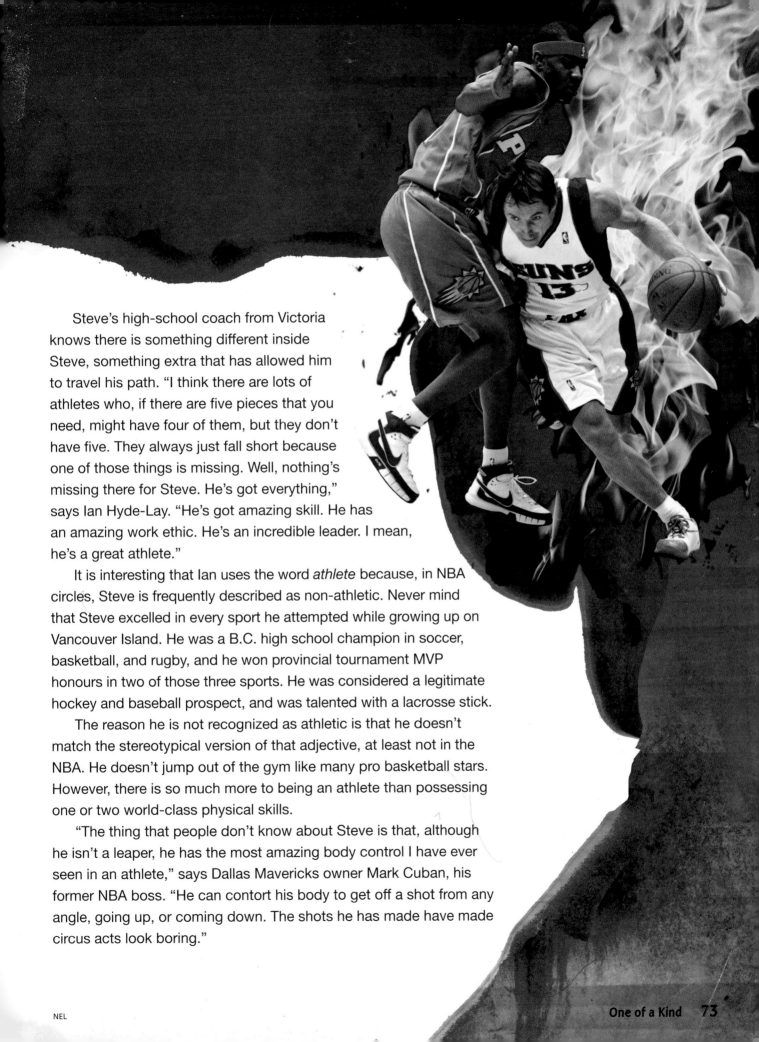

Steve's high-school coach from Victoria knows there is something different inside Steve, something extra that has allowed him to travel his path. "I think there are lots of athletes who, if there are five pieces that you need, might have four of them, but they don't have five. They always just fall short because one of those things is missing. Well, nothing's missing there for Steve. He's got everything," says Ian Hyde-Lay. "He's got amazing skill. He has an amazing work ethic. He's an incredible leader. I mean, he's a great athlete."

It is interesting that Ian uses the word *athlete* because, in NBA circles, Steve is frequently described as non-athletic. Never mind that Steve excelled in every sport he attempted while growing up on Vancouver Island. He was a B.C. high school champion in soccer, basketball, and rugby, and he won provincial tournament MVP honours in two of those three sports. He was considered a legitimate hockey and baseball prospect, and was talented with a lacrosse stick.

The reason he is not recognized as athletic is that he doesn't match the stereotypical version of that adjective, at least not in the NBA. He doesn't jump out of the gym like many pro basketball stars. However, there is so much more to being an athlete than possessing one or two world-class physical skills.

"The thing that people don't know about Steve is that, although he isn't a leaper, he has the most amazing body control I have ever seen in an athlete," says Dallas Mavericks owner Mark Cuban, his former NBA boss. "He can contort his body to get off a shot from any angle, going up, or coming down. The shots he has made have made circus acts look boring."

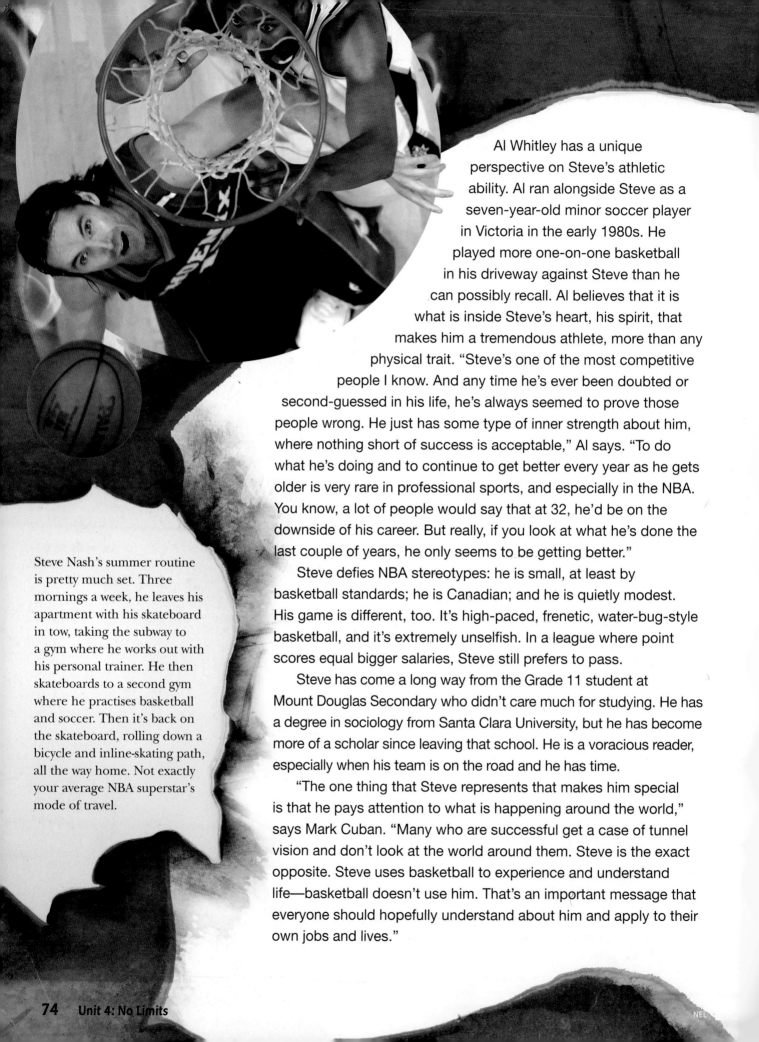

Al Whitley has a unique perspective on Steve's athletic ability. Al ran alongside Steve as a seven-year-old minor soccer player in Victoria in the early 1980s. He played more one-on-one basketball in his driveway against Steve than he can possibly recall. Al believes that it is what is inside Steve's heart, his spirit, that makes him a tremendous athlete, more than any physical trait. "Steve's one of the most competitive people I know. And any time he's ever been doubted or second-guessed in his life, he's always seemed to prove those people wrong. He just has some type of inner strength about him, where nothing short of success is acceptable," Al says. "To do what he's doing and to continue to get better every year as he gets older is very rare in professional sports, and especially in the NBA. You know, a lot of people would say that at 32, he'd be on the downside of his career. But really, if you look at what he's done the last couple of years, he only seems to be getting better."

Steve defies NBA stereotypes: he is small, at least by basketball standards; he is Canadian; and he is quietly modest. His game is different, too. It's high-paced, frenetic, water-bug-style basketball, and it's extremely unselfish. In a league where point scores equal bigger salaries, Steve still prefers to pass.

Steve has come a long way from the Grade 11 student at Mount Douglas Secondary who didn't care much for studying. He has a degree in sociology from Santa Clara University, but he has become more of a scholar since leaving that school. He is a voracious reader, especially when his team is on the road and he has time.

"The one thing that Steve represents that makes him special is that he pays attention to what is happening around the world," says Mark Cuban. "Many who are successful get a case of tunnel vision and don't look at the world around them. Steve is the exact opposite. Steve uses basketball to experience and understand life—basketball doesn't use him. That's an important message that everyone should hopefully understand about him and apply to their own jobs and lives."

Steve Nash's summer routine is pretty much set. Three mornings a week, he leaves his apartment with his skateboard in tow, taking the subway to a gym where he works out with his personal trainer. He then skateboards to a second gym where he practises basketball and soccer. Then it's back on the skateboard, rolling down a bicycle and inline-skating path, all the way home. Not exactly your average NBA superstar's mode of travel.

Steve Nash is all about assists—on the court and off. Somewhere on his way to becoming an NBA millionaire, he decided that he had a responsibility to share his good fortune. That spirit most likely originates from his parents, John and Jean, who established a warm, supportive household and taught their children to think of others besides themselves.

In 2001, Steve established the Steve Nash Foundation, a charity dedicated to "assisting underserved children in their health, personal development, education, and enjoyment of life." The foundation raised nearly $650 000 through charity basketball games in 2005 and 2006 in Toronto and Vancouver, respectively. It funds the Steve Nash Youth Basketball League in British Columbia, which now includes more than 8000 players province-wide. It has also contributed heavily to the future construction of an all-kids, all-access basketball facility in Greater Toronto.

When Steve became a wealthy young man playing in the NBA, it dawned on him: "I started to learn more about the diversity there is in the world and the inequality. It got me thinking. The NBA also does a great job in the community, trying to bring people together. With those two forces, I realized I have the potential to help people individually, and it just kind of grew."

Reflecting

Summarizing: What is this author's purpose? What text pattern does he use? How would you organize a summary of this profile?

Metacognition: How useful do you find creating a graphic organizer in helping you summarize? What else helps you summarize a selection?

Critical Literacy: In your opinion, does this text present a balanced portrayal of Steve Nash? How does the author view Steve? How can you tell?

How to ▶ Improve Word Choice

When you write your first draft, your primary focus is on ideas, not word choice. Revise your first draft to add power and interest to your writing. Improve your word choice by replacing vague or tired words with precise words appropriate to your audience, topic, and purpose.

Tips for Improving Word Choice	Sample Text
Use *analogies* (comparing one thing to another) to help readers understand words or concepts.	The jagged mountain pass reminded Cara of photos she'd seen of highways and bridges devastated by earthquakes.
Underline repeated words. If possible, replace with synonyms. Choose synonyms appropriate for your tone.	Which synonym works best in the above sample sentence: *devastated*, *destroyed*, *decimated*, *damaged*, or *ruined*?
Use strong, precise verbs that allow readers to visualize the action.	Cara slid and stumbled down the icy slope, out of control.
Use sensory words that help readers smell, taste, see, feel, and hear the scene.	The campsite was deep within an icy cavern that echoed strangely. A small campfire cast a weak light and added the smell of burning wood to the stink of unwashed climbers.
Check for words that readers might not understand. Either replace these words or provide definitions.	Cara knew that the *sastrugi* (snow eroded by the wind with a rough, sand-blasted texture) in her path might not be stable.
Delete unnecessary words that don't contribute to your message or mood, or that make the writing wordy.	Cara pushed through to the top, despite her fear, only knowing she was needed.

Vague or Tired Words	Possible Replacements
nice	wonderful, kind, thoughtful, polite
said	declared, stated, exclaimed, shouted, cried, uttered, replied

Transfer Your Learning

Across the Strands

Media Literacy : Can you think of an ad that demonstrates really effective word choices? What was it for? Why is it memorable?

Across the Curriculum

Science and Technology: When you write a science report, which of the above tips is most useful?

Talk About It

What do you think the phrase *going it alone* means?

Going It Alone

Mountain Climber Laurie Skreslet Challenges His Limits

**Nonfiction Recount
by Laurie Skreslet and
Elizabeth MacLeod from
*To the Top of Everest***

Word Choice →

Good writers use analogies to help readers understand words or concepts. This section compares the challenges of climbing a mountain to the challenges people face in daily life.

Word Choice ↘

Good writers use strong, precise verbs to help readers visualize. What does the word *barked* suggest to you?

Mount Everest is the world's highest mountain peak at about 8847 m. On October 5, 1982, Laurie Skreslet, born in Calgary, Alberta, was the first Canadian to reach the summit of Mount Everest. Laurie has participated in more than 30 expeditions and is a motivational speaker. He connects the challenges of climbing a mountain with those challenges people face in daily life.

In the following text, Laurie has just reached Base Camp, a safe spot midway up the mountain. Bill March, the team leader, is closer to the summit of Mount Everest, and in need of extra help after losing expedition members. The Icefall (Khumbu Icefall) is a dangerous area of crevasses and falling ice. This area lies between the two men.

When I arrived back at Base Camp from Kunde, I was told the Icefall had been closed. I couldn't go through? Well, maybe—maybe not. I radioed Bill.

"Laurie, it's too dangerous. Stay in Base Camp!" Bill barked. "Do NOT—"

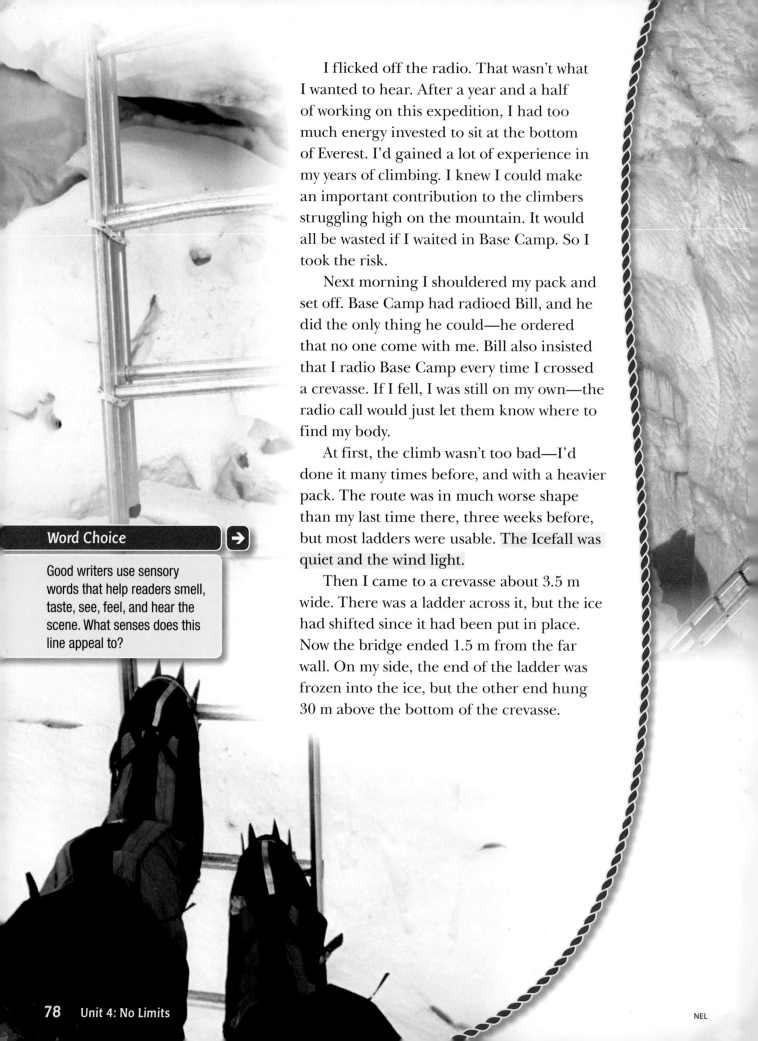

I flicked off the radio. That wasn't what I wanted to hear. After a year and a half of working on this expedition, I had too much energy invested to sit at the bottom of Everest. I'd gained a lot of experience in my years of climbing. I knew I could make an important contribution to the climbers struggling high on the mountain. It would all be wasted if I waited in Base Camp. So I took the risk.

Next morning I shouldered my pack and set off. Base Camp had radioed Bill, and he did the only thing he could—he ordered that no one come with me. Bill also insisted that I radio Base Camp every time I crossed a crevasse. If I fell, I was still on my own—the radio call would just let them know where to find my body.

At first, the climb wasn't too bad—I'd done it many times before, and with a heavier pack. The route was in much worse shape than my last time there, three weeks before, but most ladders were usable. The Icefall was quiet and the wind light.

Then I came to a crevasse about 3.5 m wide. There was a ladder across it, but the ice had shifted since it had been put in place. Now the bridge ended 1.5 m from the far wall. On my side, the end of the ladder was frozen into the ice, but the other end hung 30 m above the bottom of the crevasse.

Word Choice →

Good writers use sensory words that help readers smell, taste, see, feel, and hear the scene. What senses does this line appeal to?

I had to think clearly as I moved through the Icefall—it was extremely dangerous. (The stuff on my face is protective zinc oxide.)

← This is one of the Icefall's crevasses that I had to cross. When we originally placed this ladder it was level. The glacier raised one side of the crevasse more than 15 m!

No problem, I thought, I'll just find another place to cross.

For more than an hour, I searched desperately, but there was no other place. I had to admit defeat. Slowly, I started down to Base Camp.

Then I stopped. *Did you give that your best?* I asked myself.

Yes, I thought. But then I asked, *Did you give it more than your best?*

No, I had to answer. More than my best was to go back and jump from the ladder to the far side. I knew the impossible is often the untried. I couldn't leave without trying, so back I went.

I decided to use the handrail ropes that were still there, adding new anchors and Petzl ascenders pointing both forward and back. I figured I had a 50–50 chance of making it across.

 Word Choice

Good writers usually replace repeated words with synonyms. Why do you think the authors didn't replace the word *best* with another word?

Word Choice →

Good writers check that their writing isn't using words the readers may not understand. What jargon in this paragraph would you suggest the authors define or replace?

The ladder bobbed up and down as I edged my way out. At the end of the ladder, I focused all my concentration—and jumped.

Thwack! My ice pick bit into the ice on the lip of the crevasse. It held. I dug my crampons into the icy wall and used all my strength to pull myself up.

As I lay gasping on the far side, I realized that something powerful had happened. I seemed to be seeing things differently— everything was clearer and colours more vivid. It was like a different world. In making that leap, I'd let go not only of the ladder, but of some of my fears, too. I knew then that things would work out for me as long as I kept giving more than my best.

As I climbed to Camp One and on toward Camp Two, I thought about Bill. What would happen when I had to explain face to face why I'd disobeyed his order to stay in Base Camp? Would he allow me to keep climbing?

This photo shows Camp One as seen by Laurie as he headed for Camp Two.

"*Fear of the unknown keeps many people from achieving greatness in uncharted territory.*"
—Laurie Skreslet

Laurie took this photo of Bill at Camp Two.

He was right there when I arrived.

"Laurie!" Bill shouted. Then he smiled and said, "It's great you're here!"

"Huh?" I said, stunned by his good humour.

"Look," said Bill, "four people have died. If I'd asked you to come up and something had happened to you, I couldn't bear to have another death on my conscience. I had to tell you to stay put." Bill paused. "But I knew you'd come up no matter what. So, welcome. I need you here."

Reflecting

Reading Like a Writer: What lines in the text really help you visualize the scene and understand what Laurie experienced?

Metacognition: How does paying attention to word choice affect your appreciation of the text?

Media Literacy: If you were going to produce a movie based on this selection, what would your opening scene show? Why?

Talk About It
Do you believe that "there's nothing that you cannot do"?

A Science Mission Specialist

Mae Jemison, MD: September 1992

Poem by Bobbi Katz

"There's nothing that you cannot do."
"There's no one you cannot be."
I proved my parents' words were true.
I lived the lessons they taught me.
A child of the space age,
    beguiled by one thought:
    I want to be an astronaut!
And as I grew I kept my eyes
as the song said to do,
"on the prize ... on the prize."
First an engineer,
    then a medical degree,
next the Peace Corps
    and Africa hummed to me,
while I held the thread of a young child's thought:
I want to be an astronaut!

Now a scientist in outer space,
I've proved my parents true.
"There's no one who you cannot be."
"There's nothing you cannot do."

About Mae Jemison

Mae Jemison was born in 1956 in Decatur,
Alabama, and grew up in Chicago, Illinois.
She graduated from Stanford University with
degrees in chemical engineering and African
and Afro-American studies, and from Cornell
University with a degree in medicine. She
speaks English, Russian, Japanese, and Swahili.

Mae has had many different jobs throughout
her life: photographer, educator, graphic artist,
doctor, research scientist, and astronaut.
She has worked around the world ... and out
of this world! In 1992, for eight days in space,
Mae worked on 44 experiments as a science
mission specialist. The mission took place on
the Spacelab and was conducted by scientists
from Japan and the United States.

In 1994, Mae founded the Dorothy Jemison
Foundation of Excellence (named after her
mother). One of its projects is The Earth We
Share, an international science camp for
high-school students. Students gather and
reflect on world issues such as population. Mae
was inspired by the attitude and audacity of
Martin Luther King, Jr and she says, "The best
way to make dreams come true is to wake up."

Mae has also had a lifelong interest in
dance and has choreographed and produced
shows of modern jazz and African dance.
She considers both science and dance to be
"expressions of the boundless creativity that
people have to share with one another." Mae is
the only "real" astronaut to ever appear on *Star Trek*
(*Star Trek: The Next Generation*, an episode called
"Second Chances").

Reflecting

Reading Like a Writer: In this poem, a child's
thoughts are compared to holding a thread.
What image do you see when you think of the
comparison suggested by this word choice?
Why do you think the poet chose this comparison?

Metacognition: What strategies help you improve
your word choice when you're writing poetry?

Critical Thinking: How does this selection fit in
a unit called "No Limits"?

Talk About It
How would you answer the question in the title?

ARE YOU A RISK-TAKER?

Quiz by Brenda Zappia

Answer the questions in the following quiz to find out whether you're a risk-taker. You must answer with a *yes* or *no*, not a *maybe* or *sometimes*. So give the answer that most usually applies to how you feel.

1. Do you enjoy parties with lots of new people to meet?

2. Do you avoid people who say outrageous things just to get a reaction?

3. Do you enjoy predictable books and movies?

4. Do you participate in activities that others consider frightening?

5. Do you go out of your way to try new foods and experiences?

6. Do you prefer eating the same things or doing the same things over and over?

7. Would you ever want to climb a mountain?

8. Are your friends unconventional and outrageous?

9. When you go to the beach, do you stay close to the shore?

10. Are you positive no one could ever talk you into jumping out of a plane?

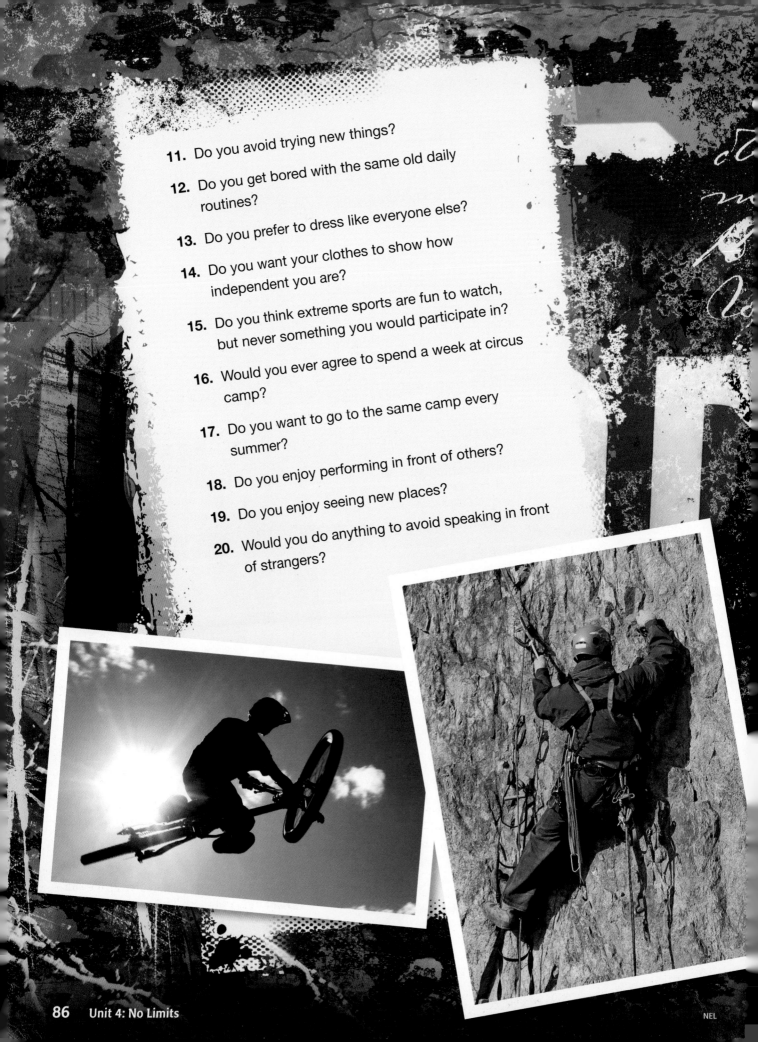

11. Do you avoid trying new things?

12. Do you get bored with the same old daily routines?

13. Do you prefer to dress like everyone else?

14. Do you want your clothes to show how independent you are?

15. Do you think extreme sports are fun to watch, but never something you would participate in?

16. Would you ever agree to spend a week at circus camp?

17. Do you want to go to the same camp every summer?

18. Do you enjoy performing in front of others?

19. Do you enjoy seeing new places?

20. Would you do anything to avoid speaking in front of strangers?

Results

Score one point for each *yes* you gave in response to numbers 1, 4, 5, 7, 8, 12, 14, 16, 18, or 19. Take away one point for each *yes* you gave in response to numbers 2, 3, 6, 9, 10, 11, 13, 15, 17, or 20.

What's your final score? If it's 10, then you're a really big risk-taker! You not only enjoy thrills and adventure, you also like new experiences, and tend to get bored with the familiar. If your score is less than 10 but more than 5, you still enjoy risk and are probably not afraid to try new things.

Remember, on this quiz, a low score doesn't mean you fail, it just means you're a cautious person who likes your usual routines.

Reflecting

Reading Like a Writer: This writer carefully chose words to create questions that you would respond to with a strong "yes" or "no." Which questions in particular did you react strongly to? Which questions did you find difficult to answer? How would you change those questions to make them easier to respond to?

Metacognition: How does analyzing the writer's choice of words affect your response to the selection?

Critical Literacy: Do you think this selection is biased in favour of risk-takers? That is, does it value risk-takers over those who don't take risks? Use evidence from the text to support your answers.

How to **Improve Understanding**

When you listen to complex oral texts (such as a group presentation, radio interview, or play), these strategies can help you improve your understanding.

Before Listening	During Listening	After Listening
• Review any handouts. Think about questions you want to ask and what you already know about the topic. • Use your prior knowledge to predict what the speaker might say. • Organize your space so that you are comfortable but not distracted.	• Make eye contact with the speaker. Watching body language and expression can help you understand what the speaker says. • Use a graphic organizer to keep track of important points. • Connect what the speaker says to what you already know. Is the speaker contradicting or confirming what you believe to be true? • Silently ask yourself questions to check that you understand the oral text.	• Ask the speaker appropriate questions to clarify your understanding. • Silently, or in conversation with others, *paraphrase* (repeat using different words) the speaker's message to confirm you understand the oral text. • Compare your understanding with that of other listeners. Listening to other people's perspectives can give you a new understanding of the oral text. • Summarize what you have heard, either orally, visually, or in writing. Ask yourself, What is the main message? How is that message supported?

Transfer Your Learning

Across the Strands

Media Literacy: Listening is as important as viewing for many media texts. Which of these tips would you use if you were viewing and listening to a movie? A documentary?

Across the Curriculum

Science and Technology: Listening is a critical skill in all subject areas. Which of the above strategies do you use most often when you are listening to a lesson in science class?

Talk About It

What major goals do you have? How do you motivate yourself to reach those goals?

MOTIVATION AND THE POWER OF NOT GIVING UP

Motivational Speech from TeensHealth

Improving Understanding

Before listening, good listeners use their prior knowledge to make predictions about what the speaker might say. What does this title tell you about the speaker's topic and perspective?

Improving Understanding

Good listeners connect what the speaker says to what they already know. What do you already know about setting goals?

→ Have you ever set a goal for yourself, such as getting fit, improving your grades, or learning a new instrument? Like lots of people, maybe you started out doing really well, but then lost some of that drive and had trouble getting motivated again.

   You're not alone! *We all* struggle with staying motivated and reaching our goals.

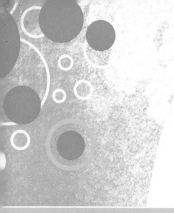

Improving Understanding →

A graphic organizer may help you to keep track of important points. What graphic organizer could help you with this selection?

Improving Understanding →

Good listeners ask themselves questions to check that they understand the text and to stay engaged. For example, here you might ask how small the small steps should be.

The reality is that refocusing, changing, or making a new start on something, no matter how small, is a big deal. **But it's not impossible.** With the right approach, you can definitely do it.

It all comes down to good planning, realistic expectations, and a stick-to-it attitude.

Here's what you need to do in **ten achievable steps:**

ONE, know your goal. Start by writing down your major goal—the *ultimate* thing you'd like to see happen. Obviously, some goals take longer and require more work than others. It's OK to dream big. That's how people accomplish stuff. You just have to remember that the bigger the goal, the more work it takes to get there.

TWO, make it specific. It's easier to plan for and master a specific goal than a vague one. Let's say your goal is to get fit. That's pretty vague. Make it specific by defining what you want to achieve (such as muscle tone or endurance), why you want to get fit, and by when. Being specific will help you make a plan to reach your goal.

THREE, make it realistic. People often abandon their goals because their expectations are *unreasonable*. Let's say you want to run a marathon. If you try to run the entire distance tomorrow without any training, you're unlikely to succeed.

FOUR, write it down, *again and again*. Research shows that writing down a goal is part of the mental process of committing to it. Write your goal down every day to keep you focused and remind you how much you want it.

FIVE, break it down. Making any change takes self-discipline. You need to pay constant attention so you don't get sidetracked. One way to make this easier is to break a big goal into small steps. Set specific daily tasks. Put these on a calendar or planner so you can check them off. Remember, reaching frequent, smaller goals is something to *celebrate*. It gives you the confidence, courage, and motivation to keep going. So reward yourself!

SIX, check in with your goal. Now that you've broken your goal down into a series of mini-goals and daily tasks, check in every day. It helps to write down your small goals in the same way you wrote down your major goal. That way you can track what you need to do, check off tasks as you complete them, and enjoy knowing that you're moving toward your major goal.

SEVEN, recommit to your goal if you slip up. **If you slip up, don't give up.** Forgive yourself and make a plan for getting back on track.

EIGHT, pat yourself on the back for everything you do right. Don't beat yourself up, no matter how far off track you get. Most people slip up when trying to make a change—it's a natural part of the process. If you keep slipping up, ask yourself if you're really committed to your goal. If you are, recommit—and put it in writing. View slip-ups as lessons and reminders of why you're trying to make a change. When you mess up, it's not a fault—it's an opportunity to learn something new.

NINE, visualize yourself achieving your goal. Self-visualization helps you keep what you're trying to accomplish in mind. It helps you believe it's *possible*. You can also call up your mental picture when your willpower and motivation are low.

TEN, positive self-talk also boosts your attitude and motivation. Or talk with a friend or even a goal buddy—someone who is trying for the same goal. Having a goal buddy can make all the difference when you don't feel motivated.

Remember, ending an unhealthy behaviour or creating a new, exciting one is all about taking **responsibility** for your life. Finding the motivation to do it isn't necessarily easy, but it is always **possible**. You can stay motivated by writing down your goals, sticking to your schedule, and reminding yourself of what led you to set your goal in the first place.

Good luck in reaching your goals!

You will achieve your goals through being too stubborn to give up.

← **Improving Understanding**

After listening, good listeners ask the speaker questions to clarify understanding. What questions would you ask about this text?

Reflecting

Improving Understanding: Other good strategies after listening include summarizing the text or comparing your understanding with someone else's. Create a three-point summary for this text. Compare your summary with another classmate's. What three points did you think were most important? What three points did your classmate include?

Metacognition: What strategies do you already use when listening to complex texts? How could you improve your listening skills?

Talk About It

Sometimes you practise something for a long time before it finally "clicks." Have you ever had that experience?

Perfecting Performance

*Evie Mark Speaks About
Throat Singing*

Interview by Bruno Deschênes

The following is an excerpt from an interview with Inuit throat singer Evie Mark from Montréal; her native village is on the north-west tip of Québec.

BRUNO DESCHÊNES: How would you describe throat singing?

EVIE MARK: Throat singing is a form of art, in a sense. It is a way of socializing. It goes like this. Two women face each other very closely and they throat sing like this. If I was with my partner right now, I would say *A*, she would say *A*, I say *C*, she says *C*. It's a sort of rolling of sounds; you create a rhythm. And the only way the rhythm is broken is when one of the two women starts laughing or if one of them stops because she is tired. It's a kind of game.

Throat singing is a very accurate technique in a sense that when you are singing fast, the person who is following the leader has to go in every little gap the leader leaves for her to fill in. For instance, if I was to say *1 + 1 + 1 + 1*, the *ones* being what I sing and the *pluses* the gaps, she would go between the *ones*, singing on the *pluses*. Then, if I change my rhythm, this woman has to follow that change of rhythm and fill in the gaps.

Throat singing is not exactly easy on your diaphragm. You are using a lot of your muscles in your diaphragm for breathing in and breathing out. Twenty minutes has been my maximum length of time to throat sing.

BRUNO: When did you start to learn to throat sing?

EVIE: I started throat singing when I was maybe 11 years old. I was raised by my grandfather and my grandmother, my Inuk side, all my life. I was always different from my friends because I was half white, half Inuk. My father is white and my mother is Inuk. I was always picked on. I wanted to prove to the society that I was as much Inuk as they were. I worked so hard at learning the Inuktituk language to prove to them that I was as Inuk as them.

There were a lot of Elders who would throat sing. It would amaze me. How could these two old women create such unique, spiritual sound? So, it became one of my goals as a young girl. And one day my Inuktituk teacher in school, a language teacher, was talking about throat singing. I went up to her and I said, "Could you teach me how to throat sing?" She said, "No problem, come over any time." Right after school, me and my best friend went to her house. She taught us a very well-known song. For the longest time, I kept practising it on my own and I'd get an itchy throat or I would start coughing. It was difficult.

I couldn't really comprehend what she was trying to teach me.

And then, one day, it just clicked. As if it was like a fishing hook, it hooked. I found what I was searching for. It was there all along. For a long period of time, I didn't practise. Maybe 10 years later I started singing again and I discovered it was still within me. And the only thing I had to work on was perfecting it.

The lady who taught me died from cancer when I was 18 and that was about the time I started performing.

It was kind of weird for me. If it hadn't been for her, I don't think I would have seen the French culture, the British culture, the Danish culture. Because of that lady, I've been able to travel around the world, even to Greenland, to share my throat singing. They don't throat sing in Greenland. They have different ways. They do a lot of drumming and spiritual sessions. Even though it is a very similar culture, people in Greenland don't throat sing anymore. I don't know when they lost it.

Reflecting

Demonstrating Understanding: How would you summarize the information in this interview?

Metacognition: Listening to two speakers rather than one can be very difficult. What strategies can you use to overcome that difficulty?

Critical Literacy: This interview first appeared in a magazine dedicated to promoting First Nation artists and art forms. What information in the interview makes that original purpose clear?

How to ➤ Analyze Point of View

Most media texts are not neutral. They reflect one or several perspectives. The people who create media texts have opinions, beliefs, and their own way of looking at the world. Often these opinions or beliefs are reflected in the media they produce.

For example, a TV news reporter broadcasts a news item about soldiers in Afghanistan. His wife happens to be serving overseas, so he ends with his own opinion about the war. The viewer hears his **point of view** as well as the background information needed to fully understand the story.

But what about other viewpoints or perspectives on this news item? There is always more than one side to any story. If the reporter included interviews with soldiers, politicians, and peace activists, then the viewer would see and have a chance to understand many points of view on the same event or issue.

Usually, news media try to be neutral and present a balanced view. However, other types of media, by their very nature, are less likely to be neutral. For example, persuasive media texts (ads and commercials) are more likely to present just their point of view, and not the viewpoint of their competitors or consumers.

point of view: The position or attitude of one person, group, or agency toward a specific topic. Also known as perspective or viewpoint. For example, a person who climbs mountains and jumps out of planes will have a different point of view about how dangerous these activities are than someone who is afraid of heights. Remember that in this situation, neither person is more right than the other; they simply have different points of view!

When enjoying media, it's important to analyze the point of view and consider whether more than one point of view is presented.

Questions	What to Look For
Does the media text have an obvious, clearly stated point of view?	Look for strong opinions or statements that clearly show how the creator(s) of the media text feel. "In my/our opinion …" "I/We believe that …" "I/We think that …"
Is there a subtle or unstated point of view?	Look for statements or messages that show a point of view without it being obvious. A TV show that depicts students involved in sports as getting poor grades may be suggesting that athletes don't do well in school.
Are different points of view presented? Does each receive equal treatment? Are all viewpoints treated with respect?	Look for ideas or issues being presented in a balanced way. Think about how much time or energy is devoted to each viewpoint and whether it is fairly represented.
Are any points of view missing? Whose viewpoint is not represented?	Sometimes what's missing tells you more than what's there about whether a text is trustworthy. Try to determine why a particular viewpoint is missing and what that tells you about the people who created the text.

Transfer Your Learning

Across the Strands

Reading: Which of the above questions are you most likely to ask when you're reading a novel or story?

Across the Curriculum

History: When you read a history text, why is it important to consider whose point of view is represented and whose point of view is missing?

Talk About It

How do you feel when someone in authority makes a decision that overturns your dreams?

OSCAR'S Olympic Dream DASHED

Analyzing Point of View →

As you enjoy media texts, analyze the point of view. From the title, whose point of view do you think will be presented in this article?

Analyzing Point of View →

Consider whether more than one point of view is presented. From the introduction, whose point of view do you *think* will be presented?

Online Article from the Associated Press, Monday, January 14, 2008

On Monday, January 14, 2008, the International Association of Athletics Federations (IAAF) ruled that Oscar Pistorius, a South African sprinter who happens to be a double amputee, couldn't compete in the Beijing Olympics. They felt his prosthetic legs gave him an unfair advantage.

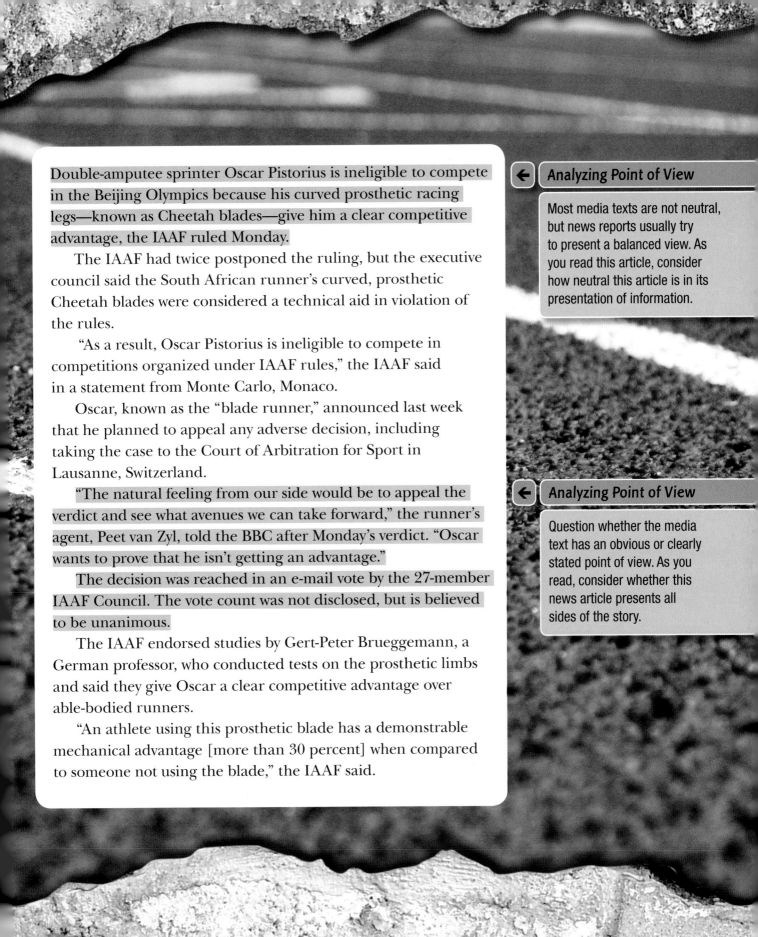

Double-amputee sprinter Oscar Pistorius is ineligible to compete in the Beijing Olympics because his curved prosthetic racing legs—known as Cheetah blades—give him a clear competitive advantage, the IAAF ruled Monday.

The IAAF had twice postponed the ruling, but the executive council said the South African runner's curved, prosthetic Cheetah blades were considered a technical aid in violation of the rules.

"As a result, Oscar Pistorius is ineligible to compete in competitions organized under IAAF rules," the IAAF said in a statement from Monte Carlo, Monaco.

Oscar, known as the "blade runner," announced last week that he planned to appeal any adverse decision, including taking the case to the Court of Arbitration for Sport in Lausanne, Switzerland.

"The natural feeling from our side would be to appeal the verdict and see what avenues we can take forward," the runner's agent, Peet van Zyl, told the BBC after Monday's verdict. "Oscar wants to prove that he isn't getting an advantage."

The decision was reached in an e-mail vote by the 27-member IAAF Council. The vote count was not disclosed, but is believed to be unanimous.

The IAAF endorsed studies by Gert-Peter Brueggemann, a German professor, who conducted tests on the prosthetic limbs and said they give Oscar a clear competitive advantage over able-bodied runners.

"An athlete using this prosthetic blade has a demonstrable mechanical advantage [more than 30 percent] when compared to someone not using the blade," the IAAF said.

← Analyzing Point of View

Most media texts are not neutral, but news reports usually try to present a balanced view. As you read this article, consider how neutral this article is in its presentation of information.

← Analyzing Point of View

Question whether the media text has an obvious or clearly stated point of view. As you read, consider whether this news article presents all sides of the story.

Analyzing Point of View →

Look for a subtle or unstated point of view. Are there any words or statements in this article that make you think the authors might favour one side over the other? Or does the article remain neutral throughout?

Point of View →

Check that different points of view are presented and that they're presented fairly and with respect. Does this article present both sides of the issue fairly? Support your response with evidence from the text.

The federation said Oscar had been allowed to compete in some able-bodied events until now because his case was so unique that such artificial prostheses had not been properly studied.

"We did not have the science," IAAF spokesman Nick Davies said. "Now we have the science. We are only interested in competitions that we govern."

Nick Davies stressed that the findings only covered Oscar's specific blades and did not necessarily mean that all lesser-abled athletes would automatically be excluded.

The ruling does not affect Oscar's eligibility for Paralympic events, in which he was a gold medallist in Athens in 2004. It remained unclear to what extent he would be able to continue running in local races in South Africa.

Underwent Testing

Oscar worked with Professor Brueggemann in Cologne for two days of testing in November to learn to what extent his prosthetic blades (j-shaped carbon-fibre extensions to his amputated legs) differed from the legs of fully abled runners.

The professor found that Oscar was able to run at the same speed as able-bodied runners on about a quarter less energy. He found that once the runners hit a certain stride, athletes with artificial limbs needed less additional energy than other athletes. As well, he found that the returned energy "from the prosthetic blade is close to three times higher than with the human ankle joint in maximum sprinting."

Based on these findings, the council ruled against Oscar.

The findings are contested by Oscar Pistorius and his team—coach, agent, manager, and other supporters.

"Based on the feedback that we got, the general feeling was that there were a lot of variables that weren't taken into consideration and that all avenues hadn't been explored in terms of coming to a final conclusion on whether Oscar was getting some advantage or not," Peet van Zyl said. "We were hoping that they would reconsider and hopefully do some more tests."

The IAAF adopted a rule last summer prohibiting the use of any "technical aids" deemed to give an athlete an advantage over another.

Needs to Qualify

Oscar has set world records in the 100 m, 200 m, and 400 m events in the Paralympics. To make the Olympics in Beijing, Oscar would still need to qualify for the South African team and make the qualifying times.

Oscar was born without fibulas—the long, thin outer bone between the knee and ankle—and was 11 months old when his legs were amputated below the knee.

He began running competitively four years ago to treat a rugby injury, and nine months later won the 200 m at the 2004 Paralympic Games in Athens.

Oscar competed in the 400 m at two international-level able-bodied meets in 2007. He finished second in a B race in 46.90 seconds at the Golden League meet in Rome on July 13 and, two days later, was disqualified for running out of his lane in Sheffield, England.

← **Analyzing Point of View**

Think about whether any points of view are missing in the media text. Does this article represent all viewpoints on this issue? If not, who is not represented?

Reflecting

Analyzing Point of View: Imagine you were writing a letter to the authors of this article. Your letter begins "I appreciated (didn't appreciate) your article on Oscar Pistorius which presented an unbiased (a biased) view of the issue ...." Take a clear position and finish this letter.

Metacognition: Which point-of-view questions helped you to improve your understanding of this article?

Critical Literacy: How would your response to this article be different if you were a member of Oscar's training team? How would it be different if you were a member of the IAAF?

Talk About It
What skills or abilities do you expect people who compete on survival-type shows to have?

Pitching a Show

Show Promotion created by Rennie Enterprises, Inc.

The following show was pitched to Canadian networks in April 2008. Does this TV show concept have what it takes to make it onto your local station?

Four teams compete to see who can conquer the Canadian wilderness, master the challenges, and find their way back to civilization, safety, and comfort. Each team consists of five players.

Some players have never seen a tree before. Others eat grubs for breakfast regularly! But who has what it takes to bring the team home? Who will win the ultimate reality show experience and a MILLION dollars?

Each week a new challenge faces *Wilderness Challenge* teams—finding water and food, making fire without matches, shooting the rapids, building an igloo or other shelter, climbing a mountain, or using the stars to navigate.

Don't Miss
Wilderness Challenge

Coming This Fall!

Here is one of the suggested posters for this reality TV show.

Over 12 weeks, contestants push their limits from the East Coast to the West Coast, ending in the Far North. Challenges take teams from rugged ocean shores to old growth forests, from northern tundra to prairie grasslands.

Each week, winning teams gain game-winning points and a survival item (fishing rod, compass, matches) that will give them an edge in the upcoming challenge! Losing teams lose points and a luxury item (toilet paper, bug spray, socks)!

Reflecting

Analyzing Point of View: What is the obvious, clearly-stated, point of view in this text? What language helps you figure out how the creators of the media text feel?

Metacognition: How does your knowledge (or lack of knowledge) about reality TV programming affect your understanding of, or response to, this text?

Critical Literacy: Who do you think might object to the use of the words *conquer the Canadian wilderness*? Why would they object?

Nonfiction Recount

When reading selections that use nonfiction recount text pattern, ask the following questions to help you make sense of the information:

- What events are being described?

- How are the events connected?

- Is each event equally important?

- In what order did the events happen?

Writers choose the text pattern they're going to use according to their purpose. If a writer wants to relate a series of events, he or she would choose nonfiction recount text pattern. A nonfiction recount describes one major event (for example, the day you climbed a mountain) or a series of related events (for example, everything that happened when you sailed around the world). You may see this pattern in history textbooks or true stories. Nonfiction recounts may be written in first person or third person.

This pattern usually

- begins with an introduction that includes background information (so that the reader knows who was involved, and when and where the events took place)

- retells events in the order in which they happened

- uses the past tense

- includes the narrator's thoughts or feelings

- gives precise details so the reader can visualize the situation

- uses dates and key words such as *after, before, finally, first, next, then, until, following, initially,* and *lastly*

Transfer Your Learning

Across the Strands

Media Literacy: Think about a movie or TV show that used this pattern. What was it about? What characteristics of the pattern did you notice?

Across the Curriculum

History: What characteristics of nonfiction recount make it an appropriate choice for a selection about the hardships experienced by settlers in Western Canada? What other text pattern might also be a good choice? Why?

Talk About It

What do we mean when we talk about an athlete having "great heart"?

Silken Laumann's Courageous Comeback

Nonfiction Recount Text Pattern

A nonfiction recount describes one major event or a series of related events. From the title, what major event do you think will be described? What do you think is the author's purpose?

Rowing to Victory
True Story by Elizabeth MacLeod

"I told the doctor who insisted that I wouldn't be able to compete in Barcelona that I thought differently."

—Silken Laumann

In early 1992, Silken Laumann was the top women's rower in the world. Everyone expected her to easily win a gold medal at the 1992 Olympics in Barcelona, Spain. Then disaster struck.

→

Born in Mississauga, Ontario, in 1964, Silken Laumann didn't always plan to be a rower. As a young child, she dreamed of being a writer. Then, when Silken was 11, she decided to be a gymnast. However, she soon grew too tall for gymnastics, so she became a runner.

Although Silken was a high-school track star, she suffered many leg and back injuries as she competed. Her sister, Daniele, who was a member of Canada's national rowing team, encouraged her to try rowing instead. "I didn't pick rowing. I think in some ways rowing picked me," recalls Silken. "Daniele was always trying to get me to row, saying this is a sport you could do really well in."

Silken was just 17 years old when she began rowing, and she quickly fell in love with the feeling of flying on water. A year later, she joined her sister on Canada's National Rowing Team and only a year after that, Silken and Daniele competed together at the 1984 Olympics. They won a bronze medal in a tough doubles race.

Accompanied by team doctor Richard Backus and her sister Daniele Laumann Hart, Silken visited the Victoria City Rowing club on Tuesday June 9, 1992.

When Daniele decided to quit rowing, Silken tried partnering with Kaye Worthington, one of Canada's best rowers. But, eventually Silken decided she would be better rowing on her own.

That was a smart decision. Silken began to win medals in top competitions around the world. In 1991 and 1992, Silken won first place in the 2000 m World Championship single sculls event. (A *scull* is a type of row boat.)

Soon Canada's female rowing team was considered one of the toughest to beat in the world. Then Silken's scull was hit in a freak accident just before the 1992 Olympics.

On May 15, 1992, Silken was in her boat warming up for a race. The Olympics were only two months away. Suddenly SMASH! Silken's scull was struck with full force by a German men's pairs boat.

"The bang, which sounded very much like two cars crashing, was my boat splintering," remembers Silken. "I didn't really feel anything, and then I looked down at my leg and it was just a mess."

Silken's lower right leg was sliced wide open. She'd broken bones and shredded muscles and nerves. Doctors told her she would probably never row again.

Was Silken's Olympic dream finished?

Silken's leg was so horribly injured that one of the men in the boat that hit her passed out when he saw it. "The injury looked so bad I actually wondered whether I was going to lose my leg, because I could see the bone," says Silken.

In a desperate effort to help heal her leg, Silken endured five operations in just ten days. Still, her doctors said that not only was her quest for another Olympic medal over forever, she would also likely never be able to row again, even just for fun.

But no one had reckoned with Silken's courage and determination.

After just three weeks in hospital, Silken insisted on being helped from her wheelchair into her racing scull. She was in a lot of pain, but she was able to row because, although her lower leg was so horribly injured, the big muscles around her hip and thigh were not badly damaged. Silken was flying on water again!

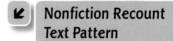

Nonfiction Recount Text Pattern

Recounts describe one major event or a series of related events. So far, this selection has described a series of related events all leading up to a few major events. How does the author signal the reader that the main focus of the selection is coming up?

Nonfiction Recount Text Pattern

Recounts usually retell events in order, using the past tense. What has happened to Silken?

Nonfiction Recount Text Pattern

Recounts usually include the author's or character's thoughts or feelings. What explicit information is given about how Silken is feeling and thinking? What can you infer about her thoughts and feelings from this paragraph?

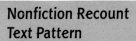

Coach Mike Spracklen helps Silken fit her injured right leg into her scull before a morning practice in Banyoles, Spain, Monday, July 20, 1992.

Nonfiction Recount Text Pattern →

Recounts usually give precise details so the reader can visualize the situation. What details help you visualize the race?

Instead of focusing on her injury or on how she had to improve to compete in the Olympics, Silken concentrated on what she could achieve each day. She still had to walk with a cane, as well as be carried and seated in her scull, and then lifted out of it after her workout. But she kept training.

"I was going hard every single day, but at that time, I was still pretty far away from the ability to go and race at an international level," remembers Silken. "Three weeks before the Olympics I was almost 30 seconds slower in my boat than I needed to be to compete at the Olympic games."

Silken persevered and when the women's single sculls final race at the Olympics was set to begin, there she was in her boat at the starting line, with her right leg heavily bandaged.

The race started well for Silken. "I competed just as if nothing had happened," she recalls. "And really, I can honestly say that for the first half of the race I felt totally normal. But then, I guess at the halfway point," continues Silken, "I really started to feel my lack of fitness, and I actually thought, I'm not going to make it."

After Silken's strong start, the American, Belgian, and Romanian rowers all pulled out in front of her. She suddenly realized she'd fallen to fourth spot.

"I just went crazy," Silken says. "I just kind of put my oars in the water and gave it everything I could for the last 20, 30 strokes of the race." She powered her way past the American boat and held on to win a bronze medal!

All across Canada, people cheered Silken and her incredible bravery, determination, and strength. Although she'd been told not to stand very long on her injured leg, she stood proudly on the Olympic podium and received her medal.

"I think that bronze medal has become something very special in my life," Silken has said, "something that represents the ability to overcome the unexpected."

Silken Laumann shows off her bronze medal at the 1992 Summer Olympic Games in Barcelona, Spain.

Silken's brave performance won her many "athlete of the year awards" in Canada. She also went on to win a silver medal at the 1996 Olympics in Atlanta, Georgia, United States.

"Rowing taught me how to take risks," reflects Silken. "It's taught me that usually a risk feels scary, but you've got to push yourself to do it. When you do," she continues, "there's a tremendous feeling of satisfaction that most things in life have a risk element to it. But that's kind of exciting and fun, and it's okay to feel afraid."

 Nonfiction Recount Text Pattern

Recounts usually use dates and key words that show the order of events. What helped you keep track of the order of events in this selection?

Reflecting

Analyzing Text Patterns: What major events were described in this selection? How were the major events connected? What helped you determine what the major events were?

Metacognition: How does analyzing the text pattern help you better understand the content of this selection?

Critical Literacy: How does this author feel about Silken Laumann? What clues in the text support your response?

Silken Laumann's Courageous Comeback

Talk About It

How do you handle the setbacks, disappointments, or even catastrophes in your life?

CHARLES MARTIN

Wheeling to the Beat of His Own Drum

Profile by Jeff Tiessen

Charlie Martin was living his dream as a rock-and-roll drummer when his life took an unexpected turn. He was hit by a car on February 22, 1977, resulting in paralysis from the waist down. After 15 years of denying the anger and heartache of his loss, he came to terms with those emotions and emerged as the man he knows he was intended to be.

"Right from the beginning and throughout my life, I have been a person who has dealt with adversity and unexpected life events. I grew up assimilating survival and coping techniques."

Charlie's Beginnings

In 1973, Charlie Allen Martin was working for $150 a week. Four years later he and his co-workers were pulling in about $1500 a week. They were members of a big-time American rock-and-roll band. Charlie was the drummer in the Silver Bullet Band that is forever linked with Detroit icon Bob Seger.

Charlie last rehearsed with the Silver Bullet Band on February 22, 1977. He was returning to his home in Detroit from the practice session in Seger's nearby hometown of Ann Arbor when he ran out of gas on the interstate. "I noticed my gas gauge was flirting with 'E' on the way to rehearsal but I was running a little late," he explains. "I completely forgot about it on the way home."

He walked about half a kilometre to a gas station. It was only 7:30 in the evening, but it was dark. As he returned to his car, his path led him across the service drive. A speeding car suddenly appeared out of the darkness. The 19-year-old driver who struck him was "impaired, uninsured, unemployed, and driving a borrowed car with no headlights," learned Charlie.

Charlie's hips and pelvis were crushed, his bladder punctured, and both femurs broken in half, among other smashed bones, but there was no spinal cord injury … initially. Charlie still twitched his legs in pain for four days after his legs were reconstructed with rods, wires and plates. Then the twitching stopped abruptly.

While there was no actual severing of or pressure on the spinal cord, the blood vessels around the spinal cord were bleeding. A clot formed, oxygen was restricted, and part of Charlie's spinal cord died.

▲ January 1977, one month before Charlie's injury

▼ Far left: Bob Seger; front left: Charlie with Silver Bullet Band

Adapting to Adversity

For Charlie, his ability to cope was never in question. He leaped right over the many stages of healing, both physical and emotional, associated with life-altering traumatic injury.

"From day one," reflects Charlie, "I've been a person used to adapting to adversity and changing situations. From the moment I was born I was taken from place to place, never knowing who to bond to or who to connect with."

While Charlie stayed away from the drums after his injury, music was his bedside companion. He had never defined himself only as a drummer. He was a singer and a keyboard player too. In fact, his mother had been a classical pianist and he followed in her footsteps at age six.

"The Beatles and Rolling Stones made piano seem a little too square for me. That's when drums became my passion. And singing has always been a primary aspect of my expression. I put drumming aside for a long time. I couldn't deal with it," he admits.

"I never went through the 'this-isn't-real' kind of denial. I knew I would never play with the Silver Bullet Band again, but I didn't stop thinking of myself as a musician. The reality of performing was in doubt, but I was still a performer," he reflects. "I'd say I skipped denial, bargaining, depression, anger, and went right to acceptance."

Charlie wasted no time in setting to work to reinvent himself as a musician. His hospital room was outfitted with a piano. He sold his drums. And before he was discharged he had been back on stage with Bob Seger and the Silver Bullet Band.

▲ August 1977, six months after the accident—special leave from the hospital

Charlie back on stage ▶

Reinventing Himself

A limousine picked him up at the hospital doors and delivered him to the concert venue where he sang and played several songs on keyboards, a request he continues to honour from his former boss and band mates whenever they're performing in southern Michigan.

Charlie explains that the challenges in his return to performing were threefold. "I had to take myself seriously. A performer is a pretty unconventional job for a musician in a wheelchair. I needed to find the courage to fantasize about performing again. Secondly, I had to get other musicians to take me seriously again—some looked at me as an image liability but the smart ones saw me as a showcase—and I had to get audiences to take me seriously," which he says, encouragingly, was the easiest of the three.

He put performing out of his mind, but set up a studio in his basement. He slowly began envisioning himself performing as a singer and piano player. Then he started flirting with the drums, modifying them so he could play again.

He ventured out to attend jam sessions. He'd sit in to sing a song now and again. He became a regular. A fan following emerged and his self-esteem was reinforced. "I began to reinvent myself as a singer," Charlie confirms. "I started to gain acceptance from fellow musicians. Eventually I started to bring my keyboards, singing and playing … performing." And then the previously unimaginable happened—he answered a newspaper ad from a band seeking a keyboard player. And soon after he was being sought out by other fellow musicians. Charlie remains a respected performer in Detroit's music scene today.

April 1985 ▲

◀ April 1985

Fortunate Variables

Not discounting music, Charlie identifies a number of other fortunate variables that contributed to his recovery. Money from Silver Bullet royalty cheques and an insurance package he bought from a musician friend just before his accident offered financial security. A supportive family that aided and adapted after his injury was key, too. And his own fortitude … "You hit the ball in the rough, you play it. Life deals you a bad set of cards, you play them out," he advocates.

Charlie confides that 15 years after his accident, he hit an emotional wall. "I could not function. I shut down. A lot of things were happening in my life then. I had lost family members. I went into a tailspin. I sought psychological counselling and found a psychiatrist who could help me release my anger and sadness. He took me back to my childhood and we addressed my disability straightforwardly. We explored my feelings about losing my job with the Seger organization. I was in denial about my pain and he helped me bring this out. It was a complete unburdening. A catharsis. I was finally able to get it out of my system. I came to see that my wheelchair is not my prison; it's my limousine."

Now 54 years of age, Charlie went back to school after his "second recovery" at age 40. He went to college to study psychology, to gain more insight into himself. He graduated with straight As and a scholarship. "Getting that degree was one of my proudest moments," he smiled.

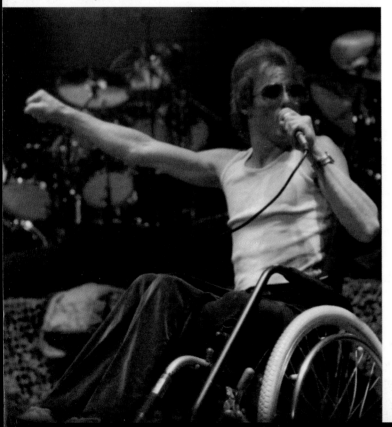

▲ April 1992

▼ April 1995

In addition to performing, Charlie also works as a facilitator in a youth assistance program. "I had a tumultuous adolescence with lots of drug use in my late teens," he divulges. "I stopped because I knew it was keeping me from my dreams. That offered me some good insight into the motivation of these kids. It's fulfilling and rewarding work. I see in every group those kids who really want to change."

Charlie reflects, "I've been in a chair for 29 years. It's hard for me to imagine being a vertical person. People say, 'You probably can't wait to be able to walk again.' And I think, 'No, why would I want that? I'd have to learn how to do everything all over again.'" As always, he wheels to the beat of his own drum.

Reflecting

Analyzing Text Patterns: What makes nonfiction recount text pattern suitable for this selection?

Metacognition: How does knowing a text pattern help you to be a more efficient reader?

Critical Literacy: What does the author, Jeff Tiessen, value? How do you know? What does Charles Martin value? How do you know?

Health

The reading strategy of summarizing can help you to better understand texts in other subject areas. As you read this article, identify its main idea and supporting details.

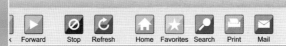

Forward   Stop   Refresh   Home   Favorites   Search   Print   Mail

Address ▼ ▶ Go

Why You're Always Tired

**Online Article
by Liz Jordan**

Do you hate to get up in the morning? Would you sleep all day if you could? If someone wakes you early, do you feel grumpy most of the day?

Of course, you probably don't find it easy to get to bed early; there's always another assignment to be done or a game of pick-up baseball to enjoy. Or maybe you find you're restless and wakeful until late in the night.

What the Experts Say

Studies of the adolescent and teen brain show that your changing sleep habits are natural. According to several experts, teens are sleepy during the day and alert late at night because an increase in growth hormones shifts their sleep/wake cycle. Everyone has an internal clock that influences sleep cycles (also called *circadian rhythms*). When you were younger, you naturally fell asleep around 8 or 9 p.m. And you naturally slept, most nights, for about 10 to 12 hours. Unfortunately, puberty has short-circuited your internal clock!

Studies show that adolescents and teens have internal clocks out of step with their earlier sleep patterns (and with the sleep patterns of most adults). In adolescents and teens, *melatonin*, a brain hormone that helps make you drowsy, is released hours later, turning you into a night owl and making it very difficult for you to be alert in the early morning.

Address ▼ Go

The Growing Brain

You're growing, and so is your brain. The thinking part of your brain, the *prefrontal cortex*, will continue to grow into your 20s. What does that growth have to do with your sleep habits? Well, during sleep, what you learned during the day is being processed by your brain.

As one expert, Dr. Carlysle Smith, explains, "We looked at students after they had finished an exam versus after they had finished just another day of school." Students' sleep patterns after the exam showed "massive increases" in rapid eye movement (REM) sleep or "dream" sleep. During that REM sleep, which occurs at the end of each sleep cycle, growth hormone is released.

To Sleep, to Dream, to Learn

During REM sleep, new brain cells and *neural connections* ("wires" which connect the right and left sides of the brain and are critical to self-awareness, intelligence, and performance) grow like branches on a tree. That means that whatever you've learned or experienced during the day becomes "hard-wired" into your brain during REM sleep.

"If you want to learn really well and be really efficient in your learning, the best way to do it is to get a good night's sleep," Dr. Smith says.

The Effects of Good and Bad Sleep Habits

Getting a good night's sleep every night not only benefits your learning, but also your health and emotional well-being. Not to mention ensuring that you're alert and able to give optimal performance during any physical task.

You need between 8.5 and 9 hours of sleep a night. Studies show that if you're NOT getting that much sleep, you're more likely to experience some of the following:

- irritability
- inability to think clearly
- poor performance in school
- higher levels of stress
- poor memory
- weight problems
- depression
- poor health (including diabetes, cancer, migraines)
- poor skin condition

And you could see how these problems might build and snowball. If you're not thinking clearly, you're more likely to do poorly in school and in other areas of your life, which may lead to higher levels of stress or depression, which may make it even harder for you to get a good night's sleep!

Resetting the Clock

So, what can you do to improve your sleep habits? Depending on whether you share a room or how quiet your home is, some of these suggestions may be more helpful than others. Do what you can to make sure you get a good night's sleep.

☑ Adjust the lighting in your room. Turn the lights down as bedtime approaches. Turn all lights off when you're in bed. If possible, make sure the lighting is bright when it's time to get up.

☑ Establish a routine. Go to bed and get up at the same time every day. End the day with a relaxing activity that helps you wind down: warm bath, reading, meditation, listening to music.

☑ Avoid caffeine. Cola, energy drinks, coffee, black tea, or chocolate during the day, but especially in the evening, will affect how well you'll sleep. Caffeine may give you a jolt of energy during the day, but for most young people, the effect of caffeine is more harmful than helpful.

☑ Avoid long naps. Too much sleep during the day will make it harder for you to fall asleep at night.

☑ Create the right atmosphere for sleep. Make your room as quiet and dark as possible. You want to be warm enough in the winter and cool enough in the summer.

☑ Avoid activities right before sleeping that increase your heart rate. You should exercise earlier in the evening (at least two hours before you go to bed). As well, try to turn off the TV or stop playing video games at least one hour before you're ready for bed.

Reflecting

Summarizing: What was this author's purpose? What text pattern did she use to suit that purpose?

Metacognition: How did summarizing this article help you understand it? What other strategies helped you?

Selections Grouped by Theme and Form

Index

Credits

Text

3–7 "Ambush" from THE THINGS THEY CARRIED by Tim O'Brien. Copyright © 1990 by Tim O'Brien. Reprinted by permission of Houghton Mifflin Harcourt Publishing Company. All rights reserved. 8 Copyright © 1996 by Jane Yolen. Published in SACRED PLACES by Jane Yolen, published by Harcourt Brace. Reprinted by permission of Curtis Brown, Ltd; and, Excerpt from *Sacred Places*, Copyright © by Jane Yolen, reprinted by permission of Houghton Mifflin Harcourt Publishing Company. 9 Mummy: from THE WAY THINGS ARE AND OTHER POEMS by Myra Cohn Livingston. Copyright © 1974 Myra Cohn Livingston. Used by permission of Marian Reiner. 10–19 From *Science Fiction Stories*, compiled by Edward Blishen, Kingfisher US, 1998. 20–23 From *My Secret Camera* by Frank Dabba Smith, photographs by Mendel Grossman, published by Frances Lincoln Ltd. copyright © 2000. Text copyright © Frank Dabba Smith 2000. Photographs copyright © Ghetto Fighters' House 1970. Reproduced by permission of Frances Lincoln Ltd. 30–31 From *So You Want to Be a Spy*, by Kate Walker and Elaine Argaet. First published in 2003 by MACMILLAN EDUCATION AUSTRALIA PTY LTD. Copyright © Kate Walker and Elaine Argaet 2003. Reproduced by permission of Macmillan Education Australia. 35–37 "Sisterly Love" from ACTING NATURAL by Peg Kehret © copyright 1991 Meriwether Publishing Ltd. Used by permissions. www.meriwether.com. 38–39 My Secret Place © 2008 by Michelle Muir. Used with permission of the author. 46–47 From "Gossip: Deal with it before word gets around" by Catherine Rondina and Dan Workman, James Lorimer & Company Ltd., Publishers. Reprinted with permission. 49–53 Reprinted with permission-Torstar Syndication Services. 58–60 From LeDREW *B.C. Science Probe 8* (c) 2006 Nelson Education Ltd. reproduced by permission. www.cengage.com/permissions. 66–69 Tanya Lloyd Kyi, *Canadian Girls Who Rocked the World*. Published by Walrus Books a division of Whitcap Books Ltd. 72–75 From Steve Nash: The Making of An MVP by Jeff Rud. Copyright © Jeff Rud 2006. Reprinted by permission of Penguin Group (Canada), a Division of Pearson Canada Inc. and Puffin Books, A Division of Penguin Young Readers Group, A member of Penguin Group (USA) Inc., 345 Hudson Street, New York, NY 10014. All right reserved. 77–81 Material from *To the Top of Everest* by Laurie Skreslet with Elizabeth MacLeod is used by permission of Kids Can Press Ltd., Toronto. Text © 2007 Laurie Skreslet. 82 Text Copyright (c) 1993, 2001, 2007 by Bobbi Katz. 89–91 "Motivation and the Power of Not Giving Up" reprinted with permission from www.kidshealth.org. Copyright © 1995–2008, The Nemours Foundation/Kids Health. 92–93 Reprinted with permission from Bruno Deschenes. 96–99 Reprinted with permission from The Canadian Press. 108–113 Reprinted with permission from Jeff Tiessen.

Photos

Cover (female runner) © Randy Faris/Corbis; (top secret) Jeff Thrower (WebThrower)/Shutterstock; (textured paper background) IKO/Shutterstock; (abstract background) andesign/Shutterstock; (abstract background) illusionstudio/Shutterstock; (speeding night traffic) Chistoprudov Dmitriy Gennadievich/Shutterstock. 1 Lee Strickland/Getty Images. 2 Christopher Meder/Shutterstock. 3–7 (background) Petrov Stanislav Eduardovich/Shutterstock; shoeberl/Shutterstock. 3 Hulton Archive/Getty Images. 5 © Tim Page/CORBIS. 7 Time & Life Pictures/Getty Images. 8–9 (blue background) iStockphoto.com/Susan Trigg. 9 iStockphoto.com/bosenok/ 20–23 (background) IKO/shutterstock; AF. Studio/Shutterstock; (barbed wire) M.E. Mulder/Shutterstock; all other photos: from My Secret Camera by Frank Dabba Smith, photographs by Mendel Grossman, published by Frances Lincoln Ltd. © 2000. Photographs © Ghetto Fighters' House 1970. Reproduced by permission of Frances Lincoln Ltd. 24 Jose Luis Pelaez Inc./Getty Images. 25–27 (silhouette) Mike Tolstoy/photobank.kiev.ua/Shutterstock; (torn paper) Mikhail/Shutterstock; (background) John Knelsen/Shutterstock. 26 Sir William Stephenson by Ronny Jaques, Macleans Magazine–Courtesy of the Camp

X Historical Society; Camp X Guard Hut by Harry Smith–Courtesy of the Camp X Historical Society. 28–29 (background) nagib/Shutterstock. 28 From www.movinghere.org.uk. 29 (George Cross) Thanks to Marion Hebblethwaite of www.gc-database.co.uk. 30–33 (background composite) Labetskiy Alexandr Alexandrovich/Shutterstock; DUSAN ZIDAR/Shutterstock; Gastón M. Charles/Shutterstock; Phecsone/Shutterstock. 30 & 31 © Bettmann/CORBIS. 34 © Mary Kate Denny/PhotoEdit Inc. 35–37 Diana Rich/Shutterstock. 38–39 (background composite) © iStockphoto.com/blackred; © iStockphoto.com/Jeanine Bremer; © iStockphoto.com/emily2K; © iStockphoto.com/Nic Taylor. 38–39 (pen) © iStockphoto.com/EuToch; Photo used courtesy of Michelle Muir. 46–47 (background) teacept/Shutterstock. 48 Digital Vision/Getty Images. 49–52 (text) Betacam-SP/Shutterstock; (blacklight device) Olivier Le Queinec/Shutterstock. 54–57 (background texture) Gordan/Shutterstock; (frame) AF–Studio/Shutterstock. 54–55 ("security") absolut/Shutterstock. 54 & 57 (spy bug/credit card) Veniamin Kraskov/Shutterstock. 55 (handprint) Mario Lopes/Shutterstock. 56 (document) Alexey Avdeev/Shutterstock; (vault 3d) AtominumeroUNO/Shutterstock. 58 (Leeuwenhoek's microscope) Utrechts Universiteits Museum/Shutterstock; (algae 10x) Harold V. Green/Valan Photos. 59 (light microscope) David Reid/Corbis Canada; (algae) D.P. Wilson/Photo Researchers Inc.; (transmission electron scope) Stanley Flegler/Visuals Unlimited; (algae) Dr. Ann Smith/Science Photo Library. 60 (scanning electron microscope) SIU/Visuals Unlimited; (algae cell) Dr. Richard Kessel/Visuals Unlimted. 61 Digital Vision/Getty Images. 66–69 (books) photogl/Shutterstock; (frame) Lou Oates/Shutterstock. 66 NAC C–009480. 67 NAC e000008477 © Canada Post Corporation (1991) Reproduced with permission. 70–71 (background) Gastev Roman. 72–75 (background composite) 7016366030/Shutterstock; Losevsky Pavel/Shutterstock; David Lee/Shutterstock; Shipov Oleg/Shutterstock; javarman/Shutterstock; SSilver/Shutterstock; Silvia Antunes/Shutterstock. 73 © Lucy Nicholson/Reuters/Corbis. 75 © Chris Coduto/IconSMI/Corbis. 77 Pichugin Dmityr/Shutterstock. 78 © Bill Stevenson/Digital Railroad 79 (on ladder) The Canadian Mount Everest Expedition; (Skreslet sitting) Bill March 80 (Camp One) Laurie Skreslet 81 (Bill at Camp Two) Laurie Skreslet; (mountains) © iStockphoto.com/Wolfgang Steiner. 82–83 (background) Mark R/Shutterstock. 83 © NASA/Roger Rossmeyer/CORBIS. 84–87 (background) Kostas Tsipos/Shutterstock; (border) AF–Studio/Shutterstock. 84 Curtis Kautzer/Shutterstock 85 (rollercoaster) Tom Hirtreiter/Shutterstock; (sushi) Nesterov/Shutterstock. 86 (bike) robcocquyt/Shutterstock; (climber) Maxim Tupikov/Shutterstock. 87 (rafting) Steve Weaver/Shutterstock; (boy playing guitar) Supri Suharjoto/Shutterstock. 88 © Bob Dammerich/PhotoEdit Inc. 89–91 (background composite) Chen Ping Hung/Shutterstock; Musha Kesa/Shutterstock; Mike McDonald/Shutterstock; (tacks) Hintau Aliaksey Leanidavich/Shutterstock. 89 & 91 ayakovlev/Shutterstock. 93 Photo: Maurizio Gatti; courtesy Evie Mark. 94 (mountains on sign) Christoprudov Dmitriy Gennadievich/Shutterstock. 95 (T-shirt) Wolfgang Amri/Shutterstock; (sky diver on T-shirt) sabri deniz kizil/Shutterstock; (climber) Danny Warren/Shutterstock. 96–99 (background composite) Ivan Cholakov/Shutterstock; Supri Suharjoto/Shutterstock; Robert Adrian Hillman/Shutterstock. 96 © Alessandro Bianchi/Reuters/Corbis. 98 © Roberto Tedeschi/epa/Corbis. 99 © Louise Gouliamaki/epa/Corbis. 100–101 (lake) Jeff Schultes/Shutterstock. 101 (compass) Colin & Linda McKie/Shutterstock; (parchment) Tischenko Irina/Shutterstock; (hiker) Galyna Andrushko. 102 © Michael Newman/Photo Edit. 103 Getty Images. 104 The Canadian Press (Bruce Stotesbury). 106 The Canadian Press (Ron Poling). 107 The Canadian Press (COC/F.S. Grant). 108–113 All photos courtesy Charles Martin.

Art

8 From SACRED PLACES, Illustrations copyright © 1996 by David Shannon, reproduced by permission of Houghton Mifflin Harcourt Publishing Company. 9 Behind the Museum Door © 2007 Lee Bennett Hopkins and illustrated by Stacey Dressen–McQueen. Published by Harry N. Abrams, Inc., New York. All Rights Reserved.